ELVIS

Portrait of the King

BY SUSAN DOLL

Publications International, Ltd.

Susan Doll holds a Ph.D. in Radio, Television, and Film from
Northwestern University. In addition to teaching film courses at several
Chicago-area colleges, she is the author of *Elvis: A Tribute To His Life,*
The Films of Elvis Presley, and *Marilyn: Her Life and Legend.* Ms. Doll
has also written for several national film publications.

TABLE OF CONTENTS

INTRODUCTION

WHAT'S IN A NAME?

—*William Shakespeare,* ROMEO AND JULIET

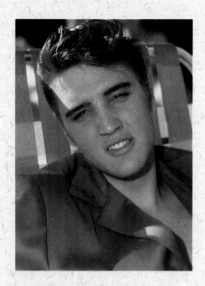

Above and below: As "the King of Rock 'n' Roll," Elvis personified the spirit of rebellious youth.

The Hillbilly Cat; Elvis the Pelvis; the King of Rock 'n' Roll; Million-Dollar Actor; the World's Greatest Entertainer.

What's in a name? The promotional monikers of Elvis Presley tell his story. They describe the different phases of his career, they reflect its diversity, and they remind fans and detractors of his enormous success and larger-than-life image.

That image evolved as Elvis's career progressed. At times, it was deliberately manipulated to appeal to a wider audience. The changes in his image are so apparent that each stage of his career marks a distinctly different Elvis Presley.

Elvis burst onto the national scene with a fury in 1956, though he had spent a year and a half performing on the country-western circuit as the "Hillbilly Cat." A new recording

contract with RCA offered widespread exposure for his music, but it was his appearances on the relatively new medium of television that made him a household name. From the time he stepped in front of the camera on *Stage Show* and launched into a manic version of "Shake, Rattle and Roll," Elvis Presley became synonymous with rock 'n' roll, rebellion, and youth gone wild.

Criticism hounded Elvis as his career began to skyrocket. Every aspect of his appearance and performance were attacked—from his long ducktail haircut to his offbeat taste in clothes to his sensual performing style. "Elvis the Pelvis" was caught up in the flurry of controversy surrounding rock 'n' roll music, and his notorious image as a dangerous rebel originated in the media condemnation that plagued him.

Through some shrewd promotional tactics by Elvis's legendary manager, Colonel Tom Parker, the negative connotation of the singer's image began to change. It didn't hurt that the entertainment press was duly impressed by the revenue that Elvis Presley generated through records, television appearances, and movies. Elvis's signature nickname, "the King of Rock 'n' Roll," supposedly came from the trade newspaper *Variety* in a 1956 article about his rapid rise through the entertainment industry. As the "Pelvis" gave way to the "King," Elvis was viewed as more than just a notorious rock 'n' roller.

A two-year stint in the army disrupted Elvis's career, but Colonel Parker turned a potentially disastrous situation into a positive career move by using his client's tour of duty

as a way to alter his image. A clean-cut, mature-looking Elvis emerged from the army to take Hollywood by storm. Concentrating on an acting career, Elvis began a schedule of starring in two to three musical comedies per year. While these films are often attacked in retrospect for their formulaic stories and mediocre songs, their box-office success made him the highest-paid actor in Hollywood in the mid-1960s. When his salary reached one million dollars per film, movie fanzines dubbed him the "Million-Dollar Actor."

While focusing on his acting career, Elvis made no concert appearances, and he limited his recording to soundtrack albums for his films. By the end of the decade, with his movie career waning, Elvis began accepting new challenges. On July 31, 1969, he performed in front of a sold-out crowd of 2,000 people at the International Hotel in Las Vegas. As his

Above left: The army helped Elvis change his image from a rebellious rock 'n' roller...
Left: ... to a romantic leading man in the movies. **Above right:** On the set of *Roustabout,* Elvis spends some time with costar Barbara Stanwyck.

band pounded out "Baby, I Don't Care," Elvis walked onstage. There was no emcee to introduce him. He grabbed the microphone, struck a familiar pose from the past, and snapped his leg back and forth almost imperceptibly. The crowd roared, jumping from their chairs to give him a standing ovation before he had sung one note. The audience whistled, applauded furiously, and pounded on the tables; some people stood on their chairs.

Encouraged by the success of this engagement at the International, Elvis returned to live performance. He was usually backed by an orchestra, a rock band, a female trio, and a gospel group, which contrasted sharply to the three-man band that accompanied him during the 1950s. The bejewelled jumpsuits that Elvis wore during this period seem a visual equivalent of the enormous sound he and his musical entourage produced. The large scale and the visual spendor lived up to Colonel Parker's favorite billing for Elvis—the "World's Greatest Entertainer."

Looking back, the various stages of his career are as distinctive as the style of music and mode of dress that characterize them. From the "Hillbilly Cat" to the "World's Greatest Entertainer," his career encompassed many changes and touched many entertainment arenas. Perhaps that is the secret of his enormous appeal: He offers something different for everyone.

Elvis Presley died in 1977, yet he continues to generate revenue for his estate, while he gains fans and confounds the media. In death, his image has become even more flexible. Fans remain loyal to a romantic idol who, for them, never ages; pop culture historians laud a legend whose contributions to popular music are immeasurable; journalists cite his drug-related decline as an example of the American Dream gone sour. The interpretations may vary widely but all are true. Even in death, Elvis means something different to everyone.

Elvis: Portrait of the King explores each phase of Elvis Presley's career as well as the key events of his personal life. His professional nicknames and personas are considered and examined to better understand how America responded to the phenomenon that was—and is—Elvis.

What's in a name? Read through these pages and discover Elvis Presley.

Opposite page: Elvis poses for a publicity shot for *Girls, Girls, Girls,* which personified the typical Presley picture. **Left:** It was during the last phase of his career that Elvis wore the jumpsuits so many people associate with him.

CHAPTER ONE

FROM TUPELO TO MEMPHIS

"WE FIGURED IF WE WENT TO MEMPHIS THERE WOULD BE MORE MONEY AND IT WOULD BE MORE FUN FOR ELVIS, BUT IN THE EARLY DAYS WE WERE BITTERLY DISAPPOINTED. HIS MOTHER AND I WALKED THE STREETS LOOKING FOR WORK. WE DID THIS EVEN IN HEAVY RAIN OR SNOW BUT FOR QUITE SOME TIME, THERE WAS NO WORK TO BE FOUND."

—*Vernon Presley*

Gladys Love Presley gave birth to twin sons, Jessie Garon and Elvis Aron, in the cold, damp predawn of January 8, 1935. Her first baby, Jessie, arrived stillborn. A half hour later, Elvis was born.

The next day, Jessie was buried in an unmarked grave in Priceville Cemetery, a few miles down the road from East Tupelo, Mississippi, where the Presleys lived. No medical evidence exists to prove that the twins were identical, yet both Elvis and his mother believed that they were. The death of his twin had a profound effect on Elvis for the rest of his life. He was both intrigued by his unknown brother and saddened by the loss of the twin he always believed was his exact double.

Confusion over the correct spelling of Elvis's middle name has existed since his birth, when the physician attending Gladys supposedly scribbled "Aaron" on Elvis's birth certificate. Photographs of a birth certificate issued by the state of Mississippi show the spelling as "Aron," which is also found on his draft notice. While in school, Elvis sometimes signed his name Elvis aron Presley, using a small "a" for "aron." His gravestone in Meditation Gardens on his estate at Graceland, however, is engraved with the more common spelling "Aaron." Biographers of Elvis Presley don't agree about the correct spelling of his middle name, though his ex-wife, Priscilla Presley—the biographer closest to Elvis on a personal level—used "Aaron" in her bittersweet chronicle of their life together.

While the truth may never be known, it is likely that Gladys intended the spelling "Elvis Aron" to match "Jessie Garon." Relatives and neighbors have said that Gladys believed throughout her pregnancy that she was going to have twins. She selected the first names of her babies to honor family members and friends. Elvis was named after his father, Vernon Presley, whose middle name was Elvis, while Jessie was the name of Vernon's father. Though the name Aron was selected to honor Aaron Kennedy, who was a close friend of Vernon's, Gladys probably chose the specific spellings of "Aron" and "Garon" because she wanted her perfectly matched boys to have perfectly matched names.

In recent years, much controversy has been generated over "Aron" versus "Aaron," resulting in outrageous speculation and exaggeration over the importance of this issue in Elvis's life and death. In a small, rural community during the Depression, where education was limited and the written word was less significant than it is now, misspellings and alternate spellings of names were typical. It was

Gladys and Vernon Presley had been married about four years when they posed for this photo with baby Elvis.

not unusual for Vernon to misspell his own name, often signing "Virnon" to important documents and records.

Vernon and Gladys Presley had been married for about a year and a half when Elvis was born. The two met in the spring of 1933, and after a whirlwind, two-month courtship, they were married. At the time of their marriage, Vernon was 17 and Gladys was 21, but they both lied about their ages on their marriage license. She said she was 19, and he claimed to be 22.

By this point in his life, Vernon had already experienced more than his share of hardships. He did not enjoy a close relationship with his father, Jessie D. McClowell Presley, who had kicked the unfortunate lad out of the house when he was only 15. Despite the friction between father and son, Vernon was his mother's favorite child. Minnie Mae Presley had four other children, but she depended a great deal on her favorite son. When Vernon moved his family to Memphis, Minnie Mae went with them, leaving the mean-tempered Jessie behind in Tupelo. Minnie would outlive both her son and her famous grandson.

Like many poor, rural Southerners during the Depression, Vernon found it difficult to land full-time employment once he became old enough to work. He worked an endless series of menial jobs to try to support himself.

Though Vernon's life until the time of his marriage was characterized by family problems and poverty, Gladys's life was just as hard. Gladys Love Smith was born in Pontotoc County, Mississippi, which was deep in the backwoods compared to the Tupelo area

where Vernon grew up. Born into a large family, Gladys shared what little the Smiths had with seven brothers and sisters. Her father, who was a sharecropper and possibly a moonshiner, died when Gladys was a teenager. She was forced to work to help support her family because her mother was frail and sick. Gladys was a tall, thin, attractive woman, with dark hair and eyes. Yet throughout much of her life, she seemed plagued by a kind of melancholy, perhaps the result of so much misfortune at an such early age.

Gladys met Vernon Presley when the Smith family moved to East Tupelo. After the couple married, Vernon built a house for his bride on land belonging to a farmer named Orville S. Bean. The two-room house was originally 15 feet wide and 30 feet long. This kind of small house is known as a "shotgun shack," because if someone fired a shotgun through the front door, the bullet would travel straight through the house without hitting anything. It is the type of rough-hewn house built for sharecroppers, usually on the property of the landowners, in a community where bullets flying through the front door would not be an unknown occurrence.

After Elvis became a star and the house became a tourist attraction, some local residents took great care to turn the shotgun shack into a quaint bungalow. They painted the outside, wallpapered the walls, and hung curtains in the windows—comforts the struggling Presley family could never have afforded. The house was also furnished with a high chair, a sewing machine, and some electric appliances, though the Presleys did not enjoy the luxury of electricity while they were living

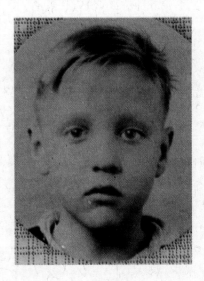

When he was a small child, Elvis resembled Gladys as a young woman.

there. A swing was added to the porch and the front yard was landscaped, but when Gladys and Vernon first moved in, the front yard was a dirt patch where Gladys kept a flock of chickens and a cow. The fresh paint and bright furnishings served to conceal the poverty in which Elvis grew up, as well as his family's meager social status. Their abject poverty was upgraded to "humble beginnings" for the sake of the tourists and the "official" Elvis Presley life story as it later appeared in newspapers and fan magazines.

Vernon Presley held a number of odd jobs before and after Elvis was born. He worked for Orville S. Bean for a time, either as a share-cropper or as an employee at Bean's dairy. He also worked at a lumber store in Tupelo, and he delivered goods for various grocery stores. In 1937, Vernon was indicted for forgery, along with Travis Smith and Luther Gable, and sentenced to three years in prison. In 1938, he was sent to Parchman Prison, which was a cotton plantation that had been turned into a prison farm where the inmates worked the land in chain gangs. Supposedly, Vernon and Smith

were bullwhipped while at Parchman. The sentence seems harsh considering the crime: Vernon, Smith, and Gable had altered the figures on a check to Vernon from Bean. No one knows the exact amount of money involved, but most people believe the sum was quite small. After his release from prison, Vernon continued to work at a variety of jobs, moving his family from relative to relative, finding permanence in neither job nor home.

Gladys began working at the Tupelo Garment Factory before her marriage, and she continued to work there until her pregnancy became troublesome. When Elvis was a few months old, she was hired to pick cotton. Unable or unwilling to find someone to care for her baby, she hauled Elvis on her cotton sack as she moved up and down the rows. After Vernon was sent to prison, Bean turned

Gladys and Elvis out of their house. They moved in with Vernon's parents, and Gladys took in laundry and worked as a seamstress to support herself and Elvis.

Though conflicting accounts of Elvis's childhood exist, all agree on one point—Gladys and Elvis were unusually close. Stories abound about Gladys's inability to leave her son in the care of anyone for any length of time. Fiercely overprotective, she was known to defend Elvis with a broom if an older boy tried to pick on him. Gladys also insisted on walking Elvis to and from school until he was a teenager. Though stories such as these are widely repeated and often exaggerated in the Elvis Presley lore and literature, few have speculated as to why Gladys was so protective of her son. Yet, a number of incidents during Elvis's childhood could easily explain her sheltering nature and the close bond between mother and child. Aside from the death of Elvis's brother at birth, Gladys suffered at least one miscarriage, resulting in her inability to have more children. As Gladys's only child, Elvis grew close to his mother, particularly during his preschool years when Vernon was away at prison. Gladys also seemed to have set goals for her son. She was determined that he would get the education that she and Vernon never had. Walking Elvis to the East Tupelo Consolidated School (later renamed Lawhon Elementary) every day assured her that her son attended school regularly.

A devastating tornado and storm on the night of April 5, 1936, may also have contributed to Gladys's special feeling about the

In this grade-school photo, Elvis (IN CIRCLE) wears denim overalls. As an adult, he despised denim jeans because they were a painful reminder of the poverty of his youth.

preciousness of her son. Elvis was just 15 months old when a tornado hit Tupelo, killing more than 200 people and injuring 500. The twister totally destroyed the neighborhood known as Tank Hill. The courthouse, many churches, and even movie theaters were converted into temporary hospitals. President Franklin D. Roosevelt sent federal aid, and the Red Cross was called in to assist people whose homes had been demolished. The Presleys, who had been at church, weathered the event at the home of Elvis's Great-Uncle Noah, along with other members of the Presley clan. The storm that followed the tornado raged into the morning hours of April 6. When Vernon and Gladys finally ventured out to return to their own home, they feared the worst. As they approached Old Saltillo Road, where their shotgun shack was located, they discovered that the tornado had flattened St. Mark's Methodist Church across the road from their house. Miraculously, it had left their tiny home untouched. At that moment, the Presleys were genuinely thankful for what little they had.

During the Depression, the people in Tupelo, like people everywhere, relied on family and neighbors for help during times of extreme economic hardship. Elvis not only felt a deep bond for his mother, but he was also close to his aunts, uncles, and cousins. After he became successful, he took care of many of them financially, just as some of them had taken care of Gladys and him during those early years.

The Presleys belonged to the First Assembly of God Church, which is a Pentecostal sect that believes in faith healing and baptism conferring the gift of tongues. Many biographers attribute Elvis's flamboyant performing style to the influence of this emotionally expressive church, although the connection may be exaggerated. Gladys recalled, "When Elvis was just a little fellow, he would slide off my lap, run down the aisle, and scramble up to the front of the church. He would stand looking up at the choir and try to sing with them." Elvis himself often referred to singing in this little church for a congregation of about 25 people, and he fondly recalled watching impassioned preachers lead services. The exact nature of the church's influence on Elvis is open to debate, though his warm recollections of watching the colorful, emotionally charged preachers suggests an inspiration of some importance.

In 1945, at the age of ten, Elvis won second place in the annual Mississippi-Alabama Fair and Dairy Show for singing "Old Shep," a ballad about a boy and his dog made popular by country singer Red Foley. Elvis's prize consisted of free passes for all of the rides at the fair plus five dollars. The show was broadcast live over Tupelo radio station WELO, marking Elvis's first documented radio performance. Young Shirley Jones Gallentine won first prize by singing a rousing rendition of "My Dreams Are Getting Better All the Time," though others have since come forward to claim that they had won the top prize on that eventful day. Elvis's teacher, Mrs. Grimes, had encouraged her young pupil to enter the talent show after hearing him sing the song in class, though it was probably the principal of East Tupelo Consolidated, J.D. Cole, who officially entered Elvis into the contest.

The Tupelo Hardware Company, where Elvis bought his first guitar, is still operating on Main Street. It maintains the atmosphere of an old-fashioned hardware store from an era gone by.

At just about this same time, Elvis received his first guitar, an event that has become so veiled in myth and exaggeration that it is more folktale than biography. The young boy was supposedly given the instrument by his parents for his tenth birthday, though other accounts claim it was for his eleventh birthday. Some have written that he actually wanted a bicycle, but his family couldn't afford one, so his mother bought him a guitar instead. F.L. Bobo, who operated the Tupelo Hardware Company where Gladys bought the guitar, insisted that Elvis really wanted a shotgun. Not surprisingly, Gladys felt that a gun was too dangerous. She compromised with Elvis and bought him the guitar. Bobo supposedly told Elvis, "You take the guitar home and learn something. Someday you may be famous." Before Bobo died, he signed an affidavit that states his version of the story. The document now hangs on the second floor of the hardware store.

Elvis learned to play the guitar from his father's brother, Vester Presley, who joined Elvis's parents in encouraging the boy's musi-

cal talent. Even before Elvis appeared at the Mississippi-Alabama Fair and Dairy Show, he had been singing with his mom and dad at churches, camp meetings, and revivals. Elvis's first biographies and album-cover notes confirm that he was singing in public by the time he was nine years old.

It's possible that Elvis also sang on the amateur radio program *Black and White Jamboree* (also called *Saturday Jamboree*) on station WELO. Named for the Black and White hardware store, which housed WELO on its second floor, the Saturday-afternoon program featured a live studio audience. Local residents were allowed to perform on the program on a first come, first served basis. Elvis attended the show regularly, and he may have sung "Old Shep" on the air when he was as young as eight or nine—before his well-documented performance at the fair.

Elvis learned about traditional country-western music from Mississippi Slim, whose real name was Carvel Lee Ausborn. Slim was a native of Tupelo, and he sang on WELO for more than 20 years. He even made a few

Above: Elvis posed for this photograph in 1948, the same year the Presleys left for Memphis. **Below:** The Presleys moved into the federal housing project at Lauderdale Courts soon after arriving in Memphis. **Below right:** Elvis plays in front of Lauderdale Courts.

recordings, including "Honky Tonk Woman," "Tired of Your Eyes," and "I'm Through Crying Over You." Slim's singing style can best be described as the traditional rural-based sound then known as hillbilly music. Elvis heard Slim perform many times on *Jamboree*, and he may have taught the boy several chords on the guitar. Elvis probably met Ausborn through the singer's younger brother, James Ausborn, who was a friend of Elvis's in junior high school. Elvis's interest in Mississippi Slim indicates that he was an aspiring performer before he moved to Memphis, and his early influences included gospel and traditional country music.

The Presleys moved to Memphis from Tupelo in September 1948, just after Elvis started high school. Vernon had worked in a factory in Memphis during World War II, but he returned to Tupelo in 1947 and went to work once again as a delivery man. Most likely, the Presleys decided to move to Memphis because Vernon couldn't find enough work to support his family in Tupelo. Elvis later

explained, "We were flat broke, man, really flat broke, and one day we just packed up and left Tupelo. Dad packed up everything we owned, loaded it all on the roof and in the trunk of our 1939 Plymouth. Then we just headed for Memphis...." Shortly thereafter, Vernon's mother, Minnie Mae Presley, joined them.

For the next four years, the Presleys lived in the slums of Memphis. After a brief stay in a one-room apartment in a boarding house, they moved into the federal housing project at Lauderdale Courts. By the end of 1952, both Gladys and Vernon were working, and the family's income exceeded the maximum allowed by the Memphis Housing Authority. The Presleys were forced to leave the housing project, but they chose to remain in the Lauderdale Courts neighborhood, where they lived until Elvis became successful and bought them a house in a better part of town.

Elvis attended L.C. Humes High School, where he majored in industrial arts/wood-shop. While he was in school, Elvis held a variety of part-time jobs to help the family make ends meet. He ushered at Loew's State Theater, worked in the table department at Upholsteries Specialities, and worked for MARL Metal Products. One summer, he labored for a short time in the hot, cramped facilities of the Precision Tool factory, along with cousins Travis, Gene, and John Smith. He was eventually fired for being underage. While in school, Elvis became a target of ridicule from some of his fellow students because of his unusual appearance. When he was 16, Elvis grew his hair longer than the other boys and greased it down with pomade. He started dressing in flashy clothes, including brightly colored shirts turned up at the collar and gabardine slacks pegged at the bottoms and ballooned at the knees. This style, which was popular in the big cities of the North, was prevalent among Memphis's black rhythm-and-blues musicians. Never a particularly popular student, Elvis did enter a talent contest during his high-school years, and he felt honored when he was allowed the show's only encore. Elvis graduated from Humes in 1953 and went to work at Crown Electric as a truck driver. Supposedly, he brought home about $41 per week.

Elvis's personal taste in clothes seemed an outward manifestation of his interest in music—particularly gospel and rhythm and blues. Elvis's musical interests and influences during this period of his life have been widely debated and disputed, but he is known to have attended all-night gospel sings in the

Memphis area and to have collected recordings by rhythm-and-blues artists. In addition, the diversity of music on Memphis's radio stations had a great deal of impact on the development of his musical style, especially stations WDIA and WHBQ. Station WDIA broadcasted music aimed at black audiences. Though owned by two white men (Bert Ferguson and John R. Pepper), WDIA was staffed with black disc jockeys who played the blues, with special emphasis on local blues performers. WHBQ was a white station that played a variety of music, but it's best remembered for disc jockey Dewey Phillips's *Red Hot and Blue* program that featured the rhythm-and-blues recordings of black artists.

Memphis was the headquarters for white gospel music in the 1950s. During 1951 and 1952, Elvis frequently attended all-night

Above: Elvis attended L.C. Humes High School, which is now a junior high. **Below:** While in high school, he worked as an usher at Loew's State, among other part-time jobs.

gospel sings at Ellis Auditorium. Male quartets most often headlined at these sings, and Elvis's favorite groups included the Blackwood Brothers and Hovie Lister and the Statesmen. The lead singer of the Statesmen was the colorful Jake Hess. Many people remember this quartet for their emotional, highly stylized manner of singing and their flamboyant wardrobes, which undoubtedly made an impression on the young Elvis.

The Blackwood Brothers attended the same Assembly of God church as the Presleys, and, along with a junior quartet called the Songbirds, they represent a significant influence on Elvis. Cecil Blackwood, the youngest Blackwood brother and a member of the Songbirds, was in Elvis's Sunday school class. After he left the junior quartet to join his brothers as part of the Blackwoods, Cecil suggested that Elvis join the Songbirds. For reasons not entirely known, nothing ever came of this opportunity.

Personal accounts of Elvis's life from family members and close friends, including Priscilla Presley and Red and Sonny West, confirm that his love of gospel music was a major influence on his musical style. But other versions of Elvis's career, particularly rock 'n' roll histories, emphasize the effect that the notorious Beale Street area had on his music and performing style. The seedy joints and small clubs of this famous stretch of Memphis were home to many well-known rhythm-and-blues musicians. According to some accounts of Elvis's life, he frequented Beale Street regularly, eventually incorporating the sound he heard there into his own.

As a teen, Elvis was close to Vernon and Gladys.

However, despite his visits to the clubs on Beale Street, it is likely that Elvis's knowledge of blues and rhythm and blues also came from listening to the radio.

Elvis was familiar with the music of some well-known rhythm-and-blues artists in Memphis, including the sounds of B.B. King, Rufus Thomas, and Big Memphis Ma Rainey. King, a disc jockey at that time, recalls meeting Elvis on Beale Street after seeing the teenager hanging around the clubs and pawn shops. Elvis bought most of his flamboyant wardrobe at Lansky Brothers Clothing Store, located at the end of Beale Street.

The country influence on Elvis's music often takes a back seat to the more colorful Beale Street stories. Aside from Elvis's personal acquaintanceship with country singer Mississippi Slim back in Tupelo, Elvis and his family often listened to Memphis's many country-western radio stations. Gladys Presley loved to listen to the radio and was a big fan of country artist Hank Snow. Elvis had grown up with country music, listening to the radio with his mother.

The style and sound of country-western music had changed by 1950. Singer Ernest Tubb, known as "the Texas Troubadour," introduced the electric guitar to the *Grand Ole Opry* during the 1940s. Also in that decade, boogie-woogie fused with country to form a more raucous country sound called "western swing." The enormous popularity of Hank Williams, whose honky-tonk style had been influenced by the blues, also affected the sound of country music. By the early 1950s, some of the fans and many members of the country-music establishment had not yet embraced these innovations, but they did provide a precedent for Elvis's music.

Elvis also admired the singing styles of such mainstream pop singers as Dean Martin and Eddie Fisher. Though the pop music establishment and the traditions of Tin Pan Alley seem diametrically opposed to Elvis's early music, he felt a kinship toward pop singers and would later profess a desire to sing in their style.

Elvis Presley's early singing and performing style was marked by a true fusion of sounds. It is this fusion of gospel, country-western, and rhythm and blues, with a little pop thrown in here and there, that makes him unique and important in the annals of popular music. To declare one musical influence as more important than another is to distort what his music actually was—a full integration of contemporary musical styles into a totally new sound.

Of course, when Elvis walked into Sam Phillips's Memphis Recording Service in 1953, no one knew that.

Elvis smiles coyly in his senior class photo from the *Herald*, the Humes High yearbook.

CHAPTER TWO

HILLBILLY CAT

"SAM [PHILLIPS] DOESN'T KNOW HOW TO CATALOGUE ELVIS EXACTLY.
HE HAS A WHITE VOICE, SINGS WITH A NEGRO RHYTHM
WHICH BORROWS IN MOOD AND EMPHASIS FROM COUNTRY STYLE.
MARION KEISKER...CALLS ELVIS 'A HILLBILLY CAT.'"

—*MEMPHIS PRESS-SCIMITAR, February 5, 1955*

The story of Elvis Presley's discovery begins with a shy, 18-year-old Elvis entering a recording studio in 1953 to cut two songs on an acetate disk at a cost of four dollars. The Memphis Recording Service was owned and operated by Sam Phillips, who had been recording rhythm-and-blues artists since 1950. By the time Elvis came to the recording studio, Sam Cornelius Phillips was known as Memphis's most important independent record producer. He had opened Sun Records in 1952 to record both R&B singers and country-western artists.

Phillips enjoyed a national reputation for discovering such talented rhythm-and-blues artists as Rufus Thomas and Junior Parker. Phillips recorded these performers for independent record companies in other parts of the United States, including Chess Records in Chicago and the Modern label in Los Angeles. Phillips financed the recording sessions; paid the musicians; recorded the artists himself, often serving as the studio engineer; and then leased the master recordings to other record companies. Phillips's reputation was built on his recordings of blues performers, but he had just begun to work with country singers when Elvis walked into his recording studio for the first time.

Rock 'n' roll folklore relates a different version of Elvis's first trip to the Memphis Recording Service. According to older, more sentimental accounts, Elvis was a talented but inexperienced singer who simply wanted to make a record for his mother's birthday. Since Gladys's birthday is in April, the timing in this version of the story is not correct, because Elvis cut that first acetate disk in the late summer of 1953. It's more likely that Elvis knew of Phillips's reputation as an independent producer and came to the Memphis Recording Service to catch his attention.

Unfortunately, on the day that Elvis decided to stop by, Phillips was not there. His tireless secretary and assistant, Marion Keisker, was running the recording studio alone. She

Above: The original Sun building at 706 Union is now owned by the Presley estate. **Below left:** Elvis and Sam Phillips (CENTER) enjoy a moment inside the Sun studio. **Below right:** Phillips's assistant, Marion Keisker, immediately recognized Elvis's talent.

noticed Elvis's flamboyant clothes and his long, slicked-back hair and engaged him in conversation. Marion asked Elvis what kind of music he sang and who he sounded like. His prophetic answer, "I don't sound like nobody," piqued her curiosity, so while Elvis was singing "My Happiness" by the Ink Spots for his acetate record, Keisker also taped him so that Phillips could hear him later.

In the early 1950s, rhythm and blues, or R&B, had evolved from a combination of urban blues and swing. It was called "race music" because R&B musicians were predominantly African-American. Phillips firmly believed that the rhythm-and-blues sound could win a mass audience. He knew that white teenagers in Memphis were listening to R&B, and he suspected this to be true in other parts of the country as well. Phillips had been known to proclaim, "If I could find a white man who could sing with the sound and feel of a black man, I could make a billion dollars." According to Marion Keisker, it was a widely known statement. Elvis's second song for the flip side of the acetate was another Ink Spots song, "That's When Your Heartaches Begin." His choice of material—two songs by the Ink Spots, an established R&B group—suggests that Elvis may have known of Phillips's statement and was hoping the producer would take notice. Phillips listened to the two songs by the unknown singer but did nothing about them, even though legend has it that Elvis's natural talent immediately blew Sam Phillips away.

Years later, after Elvis had become a major star, Phillips changed the story a little. He claimed that he was the person behind the desk at the Memphis Recording Service on that landmark day. To support his claim, Phillips pointed out that Keisker didn't know how to operate the recording equipment, so he was the only person who could have recorded Elvis. But Marion Keisker has told her account of the events many times in print and during television interviews, and, as far as anyone knows, Elvis never disputed her version.

Even though nothing came of his first session at the Memphis Recording Service, Elvis was determined to give it another shot. He returned to the recording service in January 1954 to record two more songs on acetate. He sang "Casual Love Affair" and a country tune called "I'll Never Stand in Your Way." This time Phillips worked the controls. Though he offered the young singer little in the way of encouragement, he did take down Elvis's phone number and address.

Phillips didn't call Elvis until Peer Music of Nashville sent Sun Records a demo recording of a ballad called "Without You." Phillips decided to allow Elvis to record the new ballad. Unfortunately, Elvis could not seem to master the song, so Phillips asked him to sing anything else he knew. Delighted with the opportunity, Elvis eagerly ran through his extensive repertoire of country songs and R&B tunes. Phillips was impressed enough to suggest that the hopeful singer get together with Scotty Moore, a young guitarist who played with a local country-western combo called the Starlight Wranglers.

Elvis dropped by to see Moore almost immediately. Moore recalls, "He had on a pink shirt, pink pants with white stripes down the

Above and below: Sam Phillips, who owned and operated Sun, teamed Elvis with guitarist Scotty Moore to season the young singer.

Above: "That's All Right" was backed by "Blue Moon of Kentucky." **Below:** Elvis's famous sneer is already evident in this early photo.

legs, and white shoes, and I thought my wife was going to go out the back door—people just weren't wearing that kind of flashy clothes at the time." Moore introduced Elvis to bass player Bill Black, and the three musicians spent the long, hot Memphis summer trying to find a sound that clicked.

The trio worked together in the recording studio at Sun Records instead of performing in front of a live audience. Recently developed magnetic recording tape made it possible for them to do one take of a song, listen to it, then make adjustments for the next take. Presley, Moore, and Black finally hit upon their sound while they were fooling around during a break one night. Elvis started singing Arthur "Big Boy" Crudup's blues song "That's All Right" with a fast rhythm and in a more casual style than most blues songs, and Moore and Black jumped right in. Phillips's voice boomed out from the control booth, "What are you doing?" None of them really knew. How could they? How could they know that they had stumbled onto a new sound for a new generation?

Phillips was excited about the trio's sound and recognized its potential. He asked them to refine their unique interpretation of "That's All Right," and then he recorded it. The flip side of their first record was their rendition of the bluegrass standard "Blue Moon of Kentucky," made famous by Bill Monroe and the Bluegrass Boys. Elvis's first record seemed to symbolize the roots of his musical sound; a blues song occupied one side while a country song made up the flip side.

Elvis's treatment of both songs didn't sound much like the recordings by the origi-

nal artists. His approach was far more easy going, which gave his renditions an air of spontaneity. He extracted the hard vocal delivery and the tense rhythm of Crudup's version of "That's All Right" and used a more relaxed vocal style and rhythm instead. For "Blue Moon of Kentucky," the tempo was speeded up, and two elements were added that would make Elvis's sound famous. He syncopated certain lyrics, using a sort of hiccuping sound, while Sam Phillips added a reverberation, resulting in the famous echo effect. Elvis's style became the basis of "rockabilly," a term referring to the fusion of country music (commonly called hillbilly music) with a rhythm-and-blues sound that has been relaxed and speeded up, or "rocked." The term rockabilly was not widely known until after Elvis became a household name. At the time he cut his first record for Sun, there was no term that could adequately describe his style of music. When the press attempted to explain his sound, they usually made a mess of it, often confusing their readers with inappropriate or comical comparisons to other types of music. Elvis was referred to at various times as a "hillbilly singer," "a young rural rhythm talent," a "white man...singing negro rhythms with a rural flavor," and "a young man [with a] boppish approach to hillbilly music."

Not long after Elvis's success, other rockabilly and country-western singers showed up on the doorstep of Sun Studio, hoping that Phillips could work the same magic with them as he had with Elvis. Phillips eventually recorded Johnny Cash, Jerry Lee Lewis, Carl Perkins, Roy Orbison, Charlie Feathers, Billy Lee Riley, Dickie Lee, and several other lesser-known artists. With their flashy clothes, raw sound, and fervent delivery, these singers forged a new sound and style that was intensely Southern, or "Dixie-fried." As Bill Williams, Sun Records publicist recalled, "I think every one of them must have come in on the midnight train from nowhere. I mean, they came from outer space." Yet, the influence of Sam Phillips and Sun's recording artists on the development of rock 'n' roll can never be overestimated.

Sam Phillips took a copy of "That's All Right" to popular disc jockey Dewey Phillips (no relation) for the latter's *Red Hot and Blue* radio program. Memphis's hottest jock hesitated to play the Sun recording at first because his show was usually reserved for the music of black artists, but on July 7, 1954, he played the record on the air. The station received dozens of requests for both sides of the disk, and Phillips played the two songs over and over.

After receiving 14 telegrams and almost 50 phone calls in a matter of hours, he decided to interview the unknown singer on his program that very night. Elvis was supposedly too nervous to stay at home and listen to himself on the radio, so he had gone to the movies. Vernon and Gladys dashed to the theater to pick him up, and then rushed him to station WHBQ. Dewey Phillips asked Elvis a variety of questions about his life and his interests, including what high school he had attended. This was a careful tactic on Phillips's part, for as soon as Elvis said "Humes," the audience knew that he was a white man because Humes was an all-white school at that time. In 1954, Memphis schools were not yet integrated.

"That's All Right" became a fast-selling record in the Memphis area. It was shooting

Left and far left: Memphis disc jockey Dewey Phillips of WHBQ was the first to play "That's All Right" on the radio. Legend has it that he played it 14 times during his program, receiving 14 telegrams and 47 phone calls in support.

29

up the country-western charts by the end of July 1954. On July 30, Elvis Presley made his debut as a professional entertainer at the Overton Park Shell, an outdoor stage in Memphis. Singer-yodeler Slim Whitman, riding the crest of his initial wave of popularity, headlined the bill that night. Other country entertainers, including Billy Walker, Sugarfoot Collins, Sonny Harvelle, Tinker Fry, and Curly Harris, also performed. Scotty Moore accompanied Elvis on electric guitar, while Bill Black backed the young singer on stand-up, or doghouse, bass. Elvis was so new to the music scene that one newspaper ad billed him as "Ellis Presley."

Basically a very shy 19-year-old, Elvis was as nervous as a cat for the opening show. Despite this—or, perhaps because of it—he moved constantly while he was singing. Elvis swung his hips and moved his legs in the per-

forming style that would later cause a scandal. The audience screamed enthusiastically as he danced, shook, and gyrated across the stage. When he finished, Elvis ran offstage and turned to Moore to ask what in the world the audience had been hollering at. Moore laughed, "It was your leg, man! It was the way you were shakin' your left leg."

Exactly where or from whom Elvis "borrowed" his legendary performing style has become another part of rock 'n' roll folklore. The truth is that his style, with its sensual hip movements and frenetic leg shaking, integrated all the influences on his music, including rhythm and blues, black and white gospel, and country-western music. His live act remains deceptively difficult to dissect. It was at once a hybrid of various influences as well as something unique to Elvis as an entertainer, something that differentiated him from other

Below: Elvis, Scotty Moore, and Bill Black were known as Elvis Presley and the Blue Moon Boys, though Elvis was sometimes called the Hillbilly Cat. **Below right:** At first, the trio played local clubs in and around Memphis.

rockabilly singers. In Elvis's performances, you can see a little of the white gospel singer Jake Hess of the Statesmen as well as an influence from the flamboyant preaching style of Pentecostal ministers. A witness to the musical developments on Beale Street from this era claims that Elvis got his wiggles from a black musician named Ukulele Ike, who played the blues at the Gray Mule on Beale. Though uncovering the sources of both Elvis's musical sound and his performing style is important to understand why his music was so revolutionary, it is nonetheless significant that Elvis integrated those influences into a stunning style that was ultimately all his own. When Elvis began performing for mainstream audiences, a great deal of controversy was generated about his unique performing style. Interestingly enough, at this early juncture in his career, little mention was made of his shakes and shimmies. Elvis's early publicity and promotional material simply describes him as a hot, young country singer with a crazy new sound.

Elvis's second record was released on September 25, 1954. It included an R&B tune called "Good Rockin' Tonight," first made popular in 1948 by Wynonie Harris, and a country pop song entitled "I Don't Care if the Sun Don't Shine." This record moved up the charts even more quickly than his first single. It sold 4,000 copies in the Memphis area in two-and-a-half weeks. By this time, Elvis was singing with Scotty and Bill at such Memphis night spots as the Eagle's Nest. At first, the talented newcomer made guest-star appearances with the Starlight Wranglers, but soon Elvis, Scotty, and Bill were performing on their own.

In the fall of 1954, Elvis was invited to perform on the oldest and most successful country music radio program in America, the *Grand Ole Opry*. On October 2, the Hillbilly Cat and the Blue Moon Boys—as Elvis, Scotty, and Bill had been calling themselves—drove from Memphis to Nashville to appear on the show. The audience was not enthusiastic. However, since the *Opry* had always been reluctant to accept changes in country music, including the use of electric guitars and drums, it's not surprising that Elvis's highly charged performance and blues-inspired music was not well received. At that time, there was no place for Elvis's music except the country charts, and both Elvis and Sam Phillips were perplexed and disappointed by the audience reaction to Elvis's performance. The talent coordinator of the *Opry*, Jim Denny, went so far as to suggest that Elvis ought to go back to driving a truck. Backstage after his performance, Elvis was visibly upset by the rejection of *Opry* fans and his treatment by Denny. Country star Ernest Tubb tried to console the young singer, telling him "not to worry, you have done a fine job and the audience just doesn't know."

While Elvis's failure to impress *Opry* officials and fans was a setback to his career, he still had many supporters in the country-western audience. In October, Elvis performed for the first time on the *Louisiana Hayride*, a radio program broadcast from the Municipal Auditorium in Shreveport, Louisiana. The *Hayride*, unlike the *Opry*, had always encouraged new country talent, including Hank Williams, Slim Whitman, Jim Reeves, and Webb Pierce. The Hillbilly Cat and the Blue

Above: In September 1954, Elvis's second Sun single was released. **Below:** Early on, Elvis was billed as the "freshest, newest voice in country music," though he did not sound *country*.

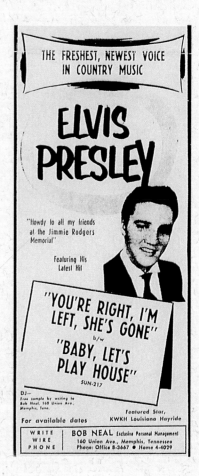

Moon Boys sang "That's All Right" and "Blue Moon of Kentucky" during the "Lucky Strike Guest Time" segment, which was devoted to new artists. The trio was so well received on the *Hayride* that they were asked back for the next week. On November 6, they were offered a one-year contract to perform every weekend. The show paid only scale wages, but it gave the trio valuable exposure to country fans outside the Deep South. Despite their contract with the *Hayride*, Elvis and his combo did not enjoy immediate fame and fortune. They continued to spend a great deal of time on the road, often performing off the back of a pick-up truck, earning a meager wage while playing the "schoolhouse circuit."

Left: Elvis and his band cut loose on the *Louisiana Hayride*. **Right:** Hayride manager, Horace Logan, chats with Elvis.

Elvis did not feel confident enough to quit his job at Crown Electric until November 1954. Vernon had always told his son that he never met a guitar player who was worth a damn, and Elvis wanted to achieve some success with his music before giving up his steady job. By that time, Elvis, Scotty, and Bill had decided it was necessary to take on the services of a professional manager. Bob Neal, a disc jockey at country station WMPS in Memphis, accepted the job and began pushing their Sun recordings, booking tours in the country-western clubs across the South and the Southwest, and handling all their business arrangements.

Bob Neal faced two problems at this time. He had trouble getting radio stations to play Elvis's records because country-western stations thought he sounded too much like a rhythm-and-blues singer, while blues stations found him too country. In addition, audiences on the smaller country circuits considered the trio's frenzied performances to be too wild. Aside from Elvis's personal performing style, bass player Bill Black liked to clown around by dancing with his huge bass fiddle or rolling across the floor with it. By 1955, these problems began to take care of themselves as Elvis's sound became more widely known as a result of his weekly appearances on the *Louisiana Hayride*. Also, his new-found fame brought the band better bookings in larger towns where their act was more acceptable. The Hillbilly Cat and the Blue Moon Boys added a drummer, D.J. Fontana, and began to appear with well-established country acts, including the Wilburn Brothers, Faron Young, Ferlin Huskey, Roy Acuff, Kitty Wells, and the Carter Family.

Left: Bill Black liked to clown around during shows by dancing with his bass fiddle. **Below:** D.J. Fontana, a staff drummer on the *Hayride,* had joined the Blue Moon Boys by 1955.

"Mystery Train" proved to be Elvis's last single for Sun.

Despite the better bookings, the Hillbilly Cat and the Blue Moon Boys continued to spend many long, hard hours on the road, travelling as far as Oklahoma for an engagement. By this time, Elvis's high-school friend Red West had joined the group as an extra driver and bodyguard. After the show, Elvis was sometimes accosted by overzealous fans, and Red was on hand to help him get to the car safely. More dangerous for the combo were the jealous boyfriends of frenzied females who had been driven to hysterics by Elvis's performance. The jilted young men were often looking for a fight, though they tended to back down when they realized they were no match for Red West.

The group usually travelled to their engagements by automobile, criss crossing the South at a surprising pace. The pace took its toll not only on Elvis and the boys but also on their vehicles. After Scotty's big Chevrolet was driven into the ground, Elvis purchased his first car—an almost-new Lincoln. Unfortunately, the car caught fire just outside Texarkana during its first road trip. Elvis and a female companion barely rescued the instruments in time before the vehicle burst into flames.

During 1955, Sun released three more Elvis singles: "Milkcow Blues Boogie"/"You're a Heartbreaker" in January; "I'm Left, You're Right, She's Gone"/"Baby Let's Play House" in April; and "Mystery Train"/"I Forgot to Remember to Forget" in August. Like his early records, these singles featured a rhythm-and-blues song on one side and a country-western tune on the other. Elvis was still considered to be a regionally based country-western per-

Elvis toured with country star Hank Snow.

former, but his popularity was beginning to soar. "Baby Let's Play House" was his first record to appear on a national chart, climbing to number ten on the country lists.

In the spring of 1955, Bob Neal booked the Hillbilly Cat and the Blue Moon Boys on a tour with country singer Hank Snow. The tour was organized by Hank Snow Jamboree Attractions, which was owned by Snow but operated by a former carnival barker named Colonel Tom Parker. Many colorful stories exist about Parker; some are no doubt true, while others have been exaggerated through the years. It's been said that he once covered a hot plate with straw and set baby chickens on top of it to make them "dance" to the tune "Turkey in the Straw." Another carny story has

Parker painting sparrows yellow and selling them as parakeets. Parker's country-western experiences included guiding country singer Eddy Arnold's career from relative unknown to star. Parker's title of "Colonel" does not refer to military rank but is an honorary title, which was bestowed upon him by the state of Louisiana in 1953. Later he was made an honorary Colonel of Tennessee as well. Much has been written about Colonel Tom Parker, not the least of which is that he is a very shrewd man.

By mid-1955, a large portion of Elvis's audience was made up of teenage girls. They were especially enthusiastic during his stage performances, and Elvis learned to play to the girls in his audience, teasing them with his body movements and making them scream each time he swiveled his hips. During a summer performance in Jacksonville, Florida, Elvis jokingly invited all the girls in the audience to meet him backstage. But the joke was on Elvis. A swarm of screaming girls chased him all the way to his car and literally ripped most of his clothes off his body. The incident terrified his mother, surprised the press, and delighted the Colonel, who had begun to monitor Elvis's career quite closely. Parker's position at Jamboree Attractions allowed him to quietly observe the young singer's steady rise in popularity.

As with other important events in Elvis's career, there are many versions of the story about how Colonel Tom Parker became Elvis's sole manager. Parker was supposed to have had a close working relationship with Hank Snow, but when he finally signed Elvis to a contract, Parker did not include Snow in the

By mid-1955, Elvis had developed a large following consisting mostly of teenagers.

deal. Parker and Snow broke up their partnership over this matter, but Snow did not sue. More sensationalized versions of the story suggest that Snow didn't sue because Parker may have had something on him; others say that Snow threatened to sue but never followed through. In 1961, Snow finally filed a lawsuit against the Colonel, claiming that he and Parker were once partners and that it was he who actually discovered Elvis.

When the Colonel and Elvis signed their first contract in August 1955, Bob Neal still had a contract as Elvis's personal manager. Parker initially signed on as "special adviser," and his specific duties were to "assist in any way possible the buildup of Elvis Presley as an artist." Parker was also given the right to negotiate renewals on all existing contracts. At

this point, Neal was kept on merely as a courtesy as he had virtually no influence over Elvis after Parker came on board. When Neal's contract with Elvis expired on March 15, 1956, he was completely out of the picture, and Parker became Elvis's full-time manager at a 25 percent cut.

The Colonel is often portrayed as the villain in the Elvis legend—a sinister, underhanded force who controlled the singer's every move and influenced his every decision. Those who see him in this light point to his background as a carnival hustler, his unsophisticated approach to promotion, and the questionable movie deals Elvis became locked into during the 1960s as proof of Parker's notorious character. In the early 1980s, information came to light that furthered this negative depiction of the Colonel. During the course of a lawsuit filed against Parker by Elvis's estate, which stemmed from a court-ordered investigation of Parker's management of Elvis, the Colonel admitted that he was not Thomas Parker of Huntington, West Virginia, but Andreas van Kuijk from Breda, Holland. This information had surfaced earlier, but Parker did not admit his true identity until it was to his advantage to do so. He used the information to declare he was not an American citizen, but "a man without a country," and therefore could not be sued under federal laws. The case was later settled out of court.

Fans and biographers continue to speculate about why Elvis let the Colonel have total control of his career. Some have suggested that because the Colonel kept "his boy" increasingly isolated from Hollywood's show business circles, Elvis knew no one who could offer

Throughout 1955, Elvis continued to tour with established country acts, including Faron Young (FAR RIGHT). About this time, Colonel Tom Parker (SECOND FROM RIGHT) became Elvis's manager.

him qualified advice on choosing scripts or song material. This made it easier for Elvis to accept the Colonel's decisions. Others have speculated that Parker was not only greedy, but he also had a desperate need for power. Controlling Elvis, who was arguably the most popular entertainer of the modern era, was Parker's way of feeling powerful. The most outrageous hypothesis, which was repeated by record producer Phil Spector and supported by some of Elvis's buddy-bodyguards, is that the Colonel actually controlled Elvis by hypnosis!

A "behind-the-scenes" opinion is given by Priscilla Beaulieu Presley in her biography *Elvis and Me.* She recalls that it was very difficult to make Parker back down. Even though Elvis sometimes complained about the ridiculous songs that he was asked to record, he stopped short of refusing to do what the Colonel wanted him to do, because he didn't want to risk jeopardizing his extravagant and often excessive lifestyle. Since both Elvis and his father hated the business part of Elvis's career and distrusted anyone associated with business, they relied on the Colonel to take care of all the details, from income taxes to contracts to career moves. According to Priscilla, Elvis would sign a contract without even reading it.

Priscilla also wrote that as Elvis grew older, he began to feel trapped by some of the Colonel's deals, particularly those involving the musical comedy films from the 1960s as well as their soundtracks. In another revealing anecdote about Parker's control over Elvis's career, Priscilla recalls how Elvis loved to harmonize with his backup groups, who were

The differences between Elvis and traditional country singers were symbolized through costuming.

Above and below: Elvis enjoys the fruits of success—devoted fans and press attention. **Below right:** Steve Sholes, an RCA executive, signed Elvis in 1955.

often gospel quartets such as the Jordanaires. On one particular album, Elvis wanted his voice to perfectly blend with those of the Jordanaires, but Parker objected, telling Elvis that his fans wanted to hear his voice loud and clear. The Colonel seemed to back down from the disagreement, allowing Elvis to record his music the way he wanted. But when the album was released, Elvis's voice was emphasized as usual. He suspected that the recording engineers were under orders to tamper with the final versions of the songs so that his voice would dominate.

Despite Parker's dubious tactics, he remains a powerful figure in Elvis's career and the motivating force behind his rise to national stardom. There is a tendency in rock 'n' roll folklore to undermine Parker's contributions by emphasizing his less-scrupulous dealings or by suggesting that Parker's control over Elvis was ultimately detrimental to his career. To do so is to misunderstand the importance of Parker's role in Elvis's fame. At the core of these harsh depictions of Parker is the suggestion that, if not for the Colonel, Elvis could have been a major figure in rock music for a longer period of time. To interpret Elvis's career in this way is to actually *misinterpret* it. Parker's master plan for Elvis was a steady pursuit of the big time, gradually encompassing larger and larger audiences in wider and wider markets. Parker's goal from the beginning was to groom Elvis to become a mainstream entertainer—a movie star and/or a pop singer. To this end, the team of Elvis Presley and Colonel Tom Parker would prove financially successful beyond their wildest expectations.

In the late summer of 1955, when Parker began to take part in Elvis's career, Elvis was just a country-western singer. Though his style wasn't traditional and many of his most loyal fans were teenagers, Elvis still toured the country circuits and performed with other country stars. His records were played almost exclusively on country stations. If Elvis was going to live up to the potential the Colonel saw in him, he was going to have to be exposed to audiences outside the South on a wide scale.

Parker's pursuit of the big time began when he negotiated a recording contract with nationally known RCA Records in November 1955. Other record companies with national distribution, including Columbia and Atlantic, were also interested in Elvis, but Parker had several contacts at RCA that made a deal with that company preferable. Sam Phillips sold Presley's recording contract to RCA for $35,000 plus $5,000 in royalties. Hill and Range music publishers paid $15,000 of the

total amount. RCA acquired all of Elvis's Sun recordings, including the unissued material, and now had the exclusive right to record him. Hill and Range received Hi-Lo Music, the small publishing company owned by Sam Phillips that was responsible for publishing the material Elvis had recorded at Sun Records.

Some critics have claimed that the quality of Elvis's music began to deteriorate at RCA. They blame the decline on commercial calculation, the tightly structured schedule for recording at RCA (compared to the makeshift, downhome atmosphere at Sun), or Elvis's own desire to follow in the footsteps of Dean Martin. Though Elvis's music did undergo some changes once he moved to RCA, the word "decline" is too harsh a word to describe the modification of his sound. Elvis's music did not decline at RCA, but it did move away from rockabilly to more mainstream rock 'n' roll. By the 1960s, it would mellow into a bona fide pop sound.

Part of the modification of his music was the result of deals Elvis and the Colonel made with the music publisher Hill and Range, which was affiliated with RCA. After the deal was finalized, Hill and Range set up two new music publishing companies: Elvis Presley Music and Gladys Music. These companies were responsbile for obtaining the rights to all the songs Elvis recorded. This set-up was financially advantageous for Elvis because he received not only his performer's royalty every time he recorded a song but also a publishing royalty. Hill and Range received half of the income generated by Elvis Presley Music and Gladys Music. The songwriters who published their songs through the two smaller compa-

nies gave up a large percentage of their royalties to the music publishers for the opportunity to write songs for Elvis. They were also required to give Elvis a cowriting credit, even though he never wrote a song or any part of a song in his entire career. But the songwriters didn't complain, because even with reduced royalties, they made a lot of money. It soon became apparent that every song Elvis recorded sold millions of copies.

Obviously, it was best for all parties financially if Elvis recorded only those songs published by his own companies, though contractually he was not prevented from recording other songs. Ultimately, the Hill and Range deal limited Elvis because the material obtained for him by Hill and Range for Elvis Presley Music and Gladys Music sometimes came from songwriting hacks who had been employed by Hill and Range for years. Any writer with an exclusive agreement for another publisher was restricted from having his work recorded by Elvis. Consequently, Elvis was sometimes saddled with lackluster material from mediocre writers.

So it was that in the late fall of 1955, Elvis began a life-long association with RCA Records and Hill and Range music publishers. Elvis was no longer affiliated with Sun Records, and his music eventually drifted away from the hardcore, rockabilly sounds that emanated from that tiny studio. Moving from hillbilly to rockabilly to rock 'n' roll, Elvis Presley stood on the brink of a phenemonal success and remarkable career. "Have you heard the news, there's good rockin' tonight"—the tag phrase of Elvis's second Sun recording—became America's wakeup call.

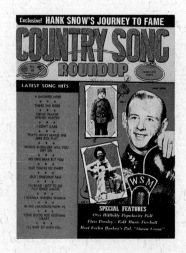

Above: *Country Song Roundup* was the first national magazine to include a feature on Elvis.
Below: Elvis named his publishing company Gladys Music after his mother.

CHAPTER THREE

ELVIS ROCKS AMERICA

"ELVIS, WHO ROTATES HIS PELVIS, IS APPALLING MUSICALLY...
THIS NEW PHENOMENON...INDULGES IN BUMPS AND GRINDS
AND OTHER MOTIONS THAT WOULD BRING A BLUSH TO THE CHEEKS
OF A HARDENED BURLESQUE THEATER USHER...."

—Ben Gross, THE NEW YORK TIMES, 1956

"WOW. I LIKE HIS ACTIONS."

—Ernestine Waynick, 14-year-old Detroit fan, 1956

"IT'S JUST MY WAY OF EXPRESSING MY INNER EMOTIONS."

—Elvis Presley

Elvis Presley burst onto the national scene in 1956 with the force of a hurricane, blowing up from the Deep South and knocking the rest of the country right off its feet. Over the course of a few weeks, Elvis was transformed from a regionally based country-western singer to a nationally known rock 'n' roll star. The speed of his transition was breathtaking, but it was no accident: Colonel Tom Parker had plans to expose Elvis to a mass audience from the beginning. It wasn't merely a case of Elvis being in the right place at the right time, as so many have assumed. When Parker signed Elvis with RCA, he also used his connections to secure "his boy" a contract with the William Morris Agency, a top entertainment-management company. Promoted by the Colonel and backed by RCA and William Morris, Elvis was introduced to a national audience by some of the giants of the entertainment industry.

Their strategy involved promoting Elvis heavily in the pop music and R&B markets as well as in the country-western market. Executives at RCA, particularly Steve Sholes, who was the head of RCA's country music division, realized that Elvis's singing and performing style differed from those of traditional country music artists. Rather than downplaying these differences, Sholes and RCA decided to exploit them in the hopes of building up Elvis's growing teenage audience. By the mid-1950s, teenagers had begun to listen almost exclusively to rock 'n' roll, and Elvis was encouraged to turn away from the country music scene to address this new audience.

While the desire to court a wider audience was the primary motivation for Elvis's shift away from country music, there was a less urgent reason as well. Conservative factions of the country music industry were beginning to resent Elvis and his new style of music. Some of the more traditional country singers took exception to following Elvis's high-voltage act when touring with him, and several Nashville music executives once requested Elvis be removed from *Billboard*'s best-selling country chart because his music sounded too much like rhythm and blues.

Two days after his birthday in January of 1956, Elvis recorded "Heartbreak Hotel," his first million-selling single for RCA. Elvis had

On January 10, 1956, Elvis recorded in RCA's Nashville studios for the first time. On that day he recorded "I Got a Woman" and "Heartbreak Hotel."

come across the song—written by Mae Axton and Tommy Durden—at a Nashville disc jockey convention the previous November. Durden had gotten the impetus for "Heartbreak Hotel" after reading a newspaper article about the suicide of a young man who had left behind a bitter note that read simply: "I walk a lonely street."

Elvis's rendition of "Heartbreak Hotel" became a nationwide hit within a few weeks. By April, "Heartbreak Hotel" was number one on many country-western and pop charts, and it climbed as high as number five on some rhythm-and-blues charts. It is a seminal record in Elvis's career not only because it was his first nationally based hit but also because it represented a step away from country music conceptually. Unlike the songs Elvis recorded for Sun Records, "Heartbreak Hotel" was a new tune written especially for him. Axton and Durden tailored the song's lyrics and its blues-influenced sound and dramatic tone to Elvis's singing style. The loneliness and alienation of "Heartbreak Hotel," coupled with Elvis's emotional interpretation, were aimed directly at his teenage audience, capitalizing on his identification with that group. Despite the move away from his previous records, "Heartbreak Hotel" recalled the Sun releases, because it borrowed the well-known echo sound, perhaps even exaggerating it.

Elvis's first RCA recording session was a familiar mix of rhythm-and-blues and country songs. In addition to "Heartbreak Hotel," Elvis recorded Ray Charles's tune "I Got a Woman" (In England, it was released on albums as "I Got a Sweetie."), an R&B song titled "Money Honey," and two new ballads, "I

Was the One" and "I'm Counting on You." Singer Kitty Wells turned the latter into a country hit later that year. The syncopation of the lyrics (the hiccuping sound) on "Money Honey" and extended guitar solos by Scotty Moore are reminiscent of Elvis's Sun recordings. These recordings also have the same basic instrumentation as Elvis's Sun releases: electric lead guitar, acoustic rhythm guitar, string bass, and drums. His first album, *Elvis Presley*, which was issued in March, combined these newly recorded tunes with some previously unreleased material purchased by RCA from Sun Records. Throughout the rest of 1956, however, as Elvis recorded more material at RCA, he moved further away from his Sun sound and its country influences, and moved closer to a fully integrated rock 'n' roll style.

Above left and above: Elvis first heard "Heartbreak Hotel" when songwriter Mae Axton pitched it to him in November 1955. Delighted with the song, he promised Axton he would record it. It became Elvis's first million-seller.

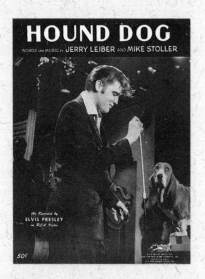

Above: "Hound Dog" was the first of Elvis's records to use the background vocals of the Jordanaires. **Below:** Elvis's first album included five songs previously recorded at Sun and seven recorded at RCA.

By the time Elvis recorded "Hound Dog" on July 2, 1956, he was seeking a bigger, more explosive sound. "Hound Dog" was originally written for blues singer Willa Mae "Big Mama" Thornton, but it had been recorded by many singers after Thornton's initial release in 1953. Elvis borrowed his version of the song from a group called Freddy Bell and the Bell Boys. He had seen the group perform the number in a club in Las Vegas and had picked up Bell's fast-paced arrangement and adopted Bell's tamer lyrics. It was Bell who added the famous lines, "You ain't never caught a rabbit. You ain't no friend of mine." "Hound Dog" became Elvis's longest-running number-one hit of 1956.

"Don't Be Cruel," another hit song that moved Elvis's musical style closer to pure rock 'n' roll, was the flip side of "Hound Dog." A relatively new tune written by Otis Blackwell in 1955, "Don't Be Cruel" had not been recorded by any singer prior to Elvis. Since the song was not associated with any singer's specific style or any particular category of music, Elvis could make "Don't Be Cruel" entirely his own. The recording's easygoing but fast-paced rhythm, light tone, and harmonious backup vocals by the Jordanaires indicate how far Elvis had drifted from the sounds of pure R&B and country music.

But, it was more than just a new promotional strategy and some minor developments in his music that transformed Elvis Presley into a rock 'n' roll singer. A vital part of that transformation occurred because of the image of Elvis that was constructed in the media at that time, particularly after his controversial appearances on television.

Two weeks after Elvis's first RCA recording session, he made his first television appearance on Tommy and Jimmy Dorsey's weekly variety series *Stage Show*. During the next eight weeks, he appeared on *Stage Show* five more times, and each time the show received better ratings. The first show, however, was only moderately successful and was beaten in the ratings by *The Perry Como Show*.

Stage Show was typical of television variety programs from the mid-1950s. Understanding the nature of variety shows from this era helps to understand why Elvis created such a stir. An hour in length, *Stage Show* featured performances by a diverse group of entertainers ranging from popular singers to animal acts to ballet dancers. Each week a guest host intro-

Elvis introduced his provocative performing style to a national audience on TV's *Stage Show*.

duced some of the acts for that particular program. On Elvis's first appearance, he was introduced by Cleveland disc jockey Bill Randle, who was supposedly the first radio personality to play an Elvis record outside the South. Randle, however, would be the only person featured on any of Elvis's *Stage Show* appearances who had any connection with the young singer. The other hosts and guest stars who eventually appeared with Elvis included jazz singers Sarah Vaughan and Ella Fitzgerald, stand-up comedians Joe E. Lewis and Henny Youngman, a chimpanzee act called Tippy and Cobina, an acrobatic team known as the Tokayers, and 11-year-old organist Glenn Derringer. In comparison to these type of entertainers—who were consid-

With each appearance on *Stage Show*, Elvis's performing style grew more explosive.

ered suitable for family audiences—Elvis's new, high-powered music and dynamic performing style seemed alien. Elvis's Beale Street clothing and ducktail haircut made the young singer stand out even further.

With each successive appearance on *Stage Show*, Elvis grew more confident and his performing style became more explosive. On his first appearance, Elvis was visibly nervous. He sang "Shake, Rattle, and Roll" and "Heartbreak Hotel," shook and shimmied to a slight degree, and then quickly moved offstage. By his final appearance, more of an interaction between Elvis and his audience took place as the young singer worked hard to drive the girls in the crowd into a screaming frenzy. When he strummed the opening chord of "Heartbreak Hotel" on his guitar, a burst of screams and applause broke out. Elvis hesitated for a moment, tantalizing the audience with anticipation. As he broke into song, he moved across the stage, shaking his shoulders and swinging his legs. Certain moves were obviously designed to illicit emotional responses from the girls, and Elvis's smiles proved he was delighted at this explosive effect on his female fans. The interaction between Elvis and his fans was very much like a game: He teased the women with his provocative moves; they screamed for more; he promised to go further; sometimes he did.

Looking back, it all seems so harmless, but Elvis appeared on the scene at a time when rock 'n' roll was coming under fire in the popular press. The controversy over rock 'n' roll centered on whether this new style of music associated with teenagers led to teenage sex and crime. During the spring and summer of

When Elvis arrived on the scene, rock 'n' roll music was not understood by the press. Offbeat stories about its impact on teenagers filled the pages of many magazines.

1956, many national magazines published articles that claimed there was a link between rock 'n' roll and juvenile delinquency. At the same time, Elvis was often featured in these same magazines in articles that sensationalized the effect of his sensual performing style on teenage girls. Headlines glared, "Presley's Impact Piles Up Fans, Fads—and Fear," while trumped up stories declared his "sex-hot flame" to be inextinguishable. It did not take a great leap of imagination for journalists, reviewers, and critics to relate Elvis's personal appearance and sensual performing style to the decadency of rock 'n' roll and the horrors of juvenile delinquency.

When the popular press was not openly criticizing Elvis, they were ridiculing him. Despite the fact that his music was identified as rock 'n' roll, journalists and reporters often referred to him disparagingly as a "hillbilly singer." He was maligned for his Southern accent, his flashy clothes, his long sideburns,

and his ducktail haircut so heavily laden with pomade that his blond hair looked black. The latter in particular seemed to raise the ire of the press and public alike. Never before had an entertainer's hair been the subject of so much attention; Elvis's hairstyle was criticized because of its length, its use of pomade, and the fact that so many teenagers emulated it.

Between television appearances and recording sessions, Elvis continued to tour the South and Southwest. Along with Scotty Moore, Bill Black, and D.J. Fontana, he kept up a breakneck pace. The group was no longer known as the Hillbilly Cat and the Blue Moon Boys but simply referred to as "Elvis Presley," with no acknowledgement of the rest of the band. By this time, Elvis's appearances at the *Louisiana Hayride* every Saturday night were

Below and below right: The reaction of teenage girls to Elvis's sensual performing style roused the anger of the PTA, civic groups, church leaders, and the mainstream press.

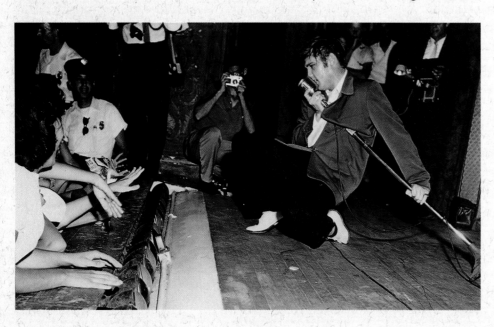

actually hindering his career, rather than helping it. Despite Elvis's new RCA contract and his ever-growing popularity, the *Hayride* was still paying Elvis and his band based on their 1954 contract. In addition, their weekly *Hayride* appearances prevented the combo from taking extensive engagements elsewhere. After much negotiation, Colonel Parker finally got Elvis released from the contract in March of 1956 for a cool $10,000, plus an agreement to make a special *Hayride* appearance sometime in the future.

In April 1956, the Colonel booked Elvis into a two-week engagement at the New Frontier Hotel in Las Vegas, a venture that turned out to be a disaster. Perhaps Parker should have known better than to book Elvis into a major engagement outside the South with an audience made up mostly of adults. After a few performances, Elvis was bumped to second billing in favor of a more typical Vegas entertainer, comedian Shecky Green. Stung by the rejection, Elvis would remember his failure in Las Vegas for many years. However, one good thing did emerge from the Vegas trip: Elvis was introduced to "Hound Dog" when he saw Freddie Bell and the Bellboys perform the song in the hotel lounge. "Hound Dog" became Elvis's signature song in 1956, ultimately bringing him as much controversy as fame.

In the late spring of 1956, Elvis appeared on *The Milton Berle Show* for the first time. The show was broadcast from the USS *Hancock*, which was docked at the San Diego Naval Station. Despite the novel location, this television appearance is barely mentioned in biographies or other accounts of Elvis's career,

Left: Elvis and manager Colonel Tom Parker pose for publicity for Elvis's first Las Vegas appearance. **Below:** Elvis's act was not well received in Vegas, but judging from this photo, his visit was not entirely disappointing.

because his second appearance on the Berle program has completely overshadowed it. It was this second appearance on June 5, 1956, that fanned the flames of the nationwide controversy over his hip-swiveling performing style. Elvis sang "Hound Dog" for the first time on television that June night. When he began the song, no one knew what to expect, since the tune was new. But the audience responded immediately with enthusiasm. Elvis then went a bit further in his performance. He slowed down the final chorus of the song to a blues tempo, and he thrust his pelvis to the beat of the music in a particularly suggestive manner. The studio audience went wild with excitement.

The next day, newspaper critics outdid one another in expressing their outrage over Elvis's television performance. Many described his act by comparing it to a striptease. Jack Gould of *The New York Times* declared, "Mr. Presley has no discernible singing ability," while John Crosby of the *New York Herald Tribune* called Elvis "unspeakably untalented and vulgar." The criticism prompted parents, religious groups from the North and South, and the Parent-Teacher Association to condemn Elvis and rock 'n' roll music by associating both with juvenile delinquency. Elvis

Below: On Elvis's second appearance on *The Milton Berle Show,* he sang "I Want You, I Need You, I Love You" with the Jordanaires. **Below right:** But, it was his inflammatory rendition of "Hound Dog" that caused a show-business scandal.

could not understand what all of the fuss was about: "It's only music. In a lot of papers, they say that rock 'n' roll is a big influence on juvenile delinquency. I don't think that it is. I don't see how music has anything to do with it at all.... I've been blamed for just about everything wrong in this country."

After Milton Berle's show, Colonel Parker booked Elvis on *The Steve Allen Show*, a new variety program that aired at the same time as Ed Sullivan's immensely popular show. Allen hated rock 'n' roll, but he was aware of the high ratings Berle's show received when Elvis appeared. He was also aware of the controversy. To tone down Elvis's sexy performance, Allen insisted that he wear a tuxedo during his segment, and he introduced him as "the new Elvis Presley." Elvis sang one of his latest singles, a slow but hard-driving ballad called "I Want You, I Need You, I Love You." Immediately after that number, the curtain opened to reveal a cuddly basset hound sitting on top of a tall wooden stool. Elvis sang "Hound Dog" to the docile creature, which upstaged the singer with his sad-eyed expressions. Allen used humor to cool down Elvis's sensual performing style, prohibiting him from moving around much on stage and even preventing him from wearing his trademark Beale Street clothes. The fans were furious, and they picketed NBC-TV studios the next morning with placards that read, "We want the gyratin' Elvis."

Later in the program, Elvis joined Allen, Imogene Coca, and fellow Southerner Andy Griffith in a comedy sketch that satirized country-western programs not unlike the *Louisiana Hayride*. Many of the jokes were condescending toward Southern culture. Allen's presentation of Elvis singing to a dog plus the appearance of the "hayseed" sketch actually ridiculed Elvis. Steve Allen was the real winner that night, because his show beat Sullivan in the ratings but generated little controversy.

Elvis had established himself as an entertainer who could attract a large television audience and boost ratings, so it's not surprising that after many rejections, the Colonel finally arranged for Elvis to appear on *The Ed Sullivan Show*, a highly rated, prime-time variety program. Sullivan, who was a powerful figure in the industry, had stated publicly that he would not allow Elvis to appear on his show because it was a *family* program. But

Above: Irish McCalla, star of *Sheena, Queen of the Jungle*, appeared on the Berle show with Elvis. **Left:** Elvis rehearses for his appearance on *The Steve Allen Show*, in which he sang "Hound Dog" to Sherlock, a basset hound.

Above and right: After declaring that Elvis Presley would never appear on his program, Ed Sullivan backed down and signed Elvis for three shows.

ratings speak louder than scruples, and Sullivan backed down from this stance after *The Steve Allen Show* was so successful. Elvis was paid an unprecedented fee of $50,000 for three appearances on *The Ed Sullivan Show*. This was a lot more than the $5,000 per show Colonel Parker had asked for only a few weeks earlier when Sullivan turned him down.

Elvis's performance on *The Ed Sullivan Show* has gone down in the annals of rock music history because of the censors' decision to shoot the volatile young singer only from the waist up. Contrary to popular belief, however, this decision was not made until his third appearance! Actor Charles Laughton served as substitute host the night of Elvis's first appearance because Sullivan was recuperating from an auto accident. In kinescopes and video footage of that performance, Elvis can be seen in full figure, crooning "Love Me Tender" and "Don't Be Cruel," then later belting out "Hound Dog" and "Ready Teddy."

Elvis's third and final appearance on Sullivan's show on January 6, 1957, contains the legendary moments when the CBS censors would not allow his entire body to be shown. Seen only from the waist up, Elvis still put on an exciting show, singing seven songs in three segments interspersed throughout the show. In one segment, Elvis and the Jordanaires sang "Peace in the Valley," which Elvis dedicated to the earthquake victims of Eastern Europe. But it was his rendition of such Presley hits as "Heartbreak Hotel" and "Hound Dog" that stirred up the studio audience. Their screams and applause clued the television viewers into what Elvis was doing out of camera range, almost subverting the censors' intent. Once again, the interaction between Elvis and the studio audience added to the power of his performance. After Elvis's final number, Sullivan declared him to be "a real decent, fine boy"—a rather hypocritical statement considering what he and the censors had just done to Elvis's act.

For years people have wondered why Elvis was censored during his *third* appearance on Sullivan's show. The simplest and most probable explanation is that Sullivan received negative criticism about Elvis's earlier appearances. Other, more outrageous explanations include the theory that the Colonel forced Sullivan to apologize publicly for remarks he'd made about Elvis to the press during the previous summer, and the waist-up-only order was Sullivan's way of getting back at Parker. The wildest explanation was offered by a former director of *The Ed Sullivan Show*, who said that during his second appearance, Elvis put a cardboard tube down the front of his

trousers and manipulated it to make the studio audience scream. To avoid a repeated occurence of that behavior, Sullivan supposedly insisted on the above-the-waist coverage for Elvis's final appearance. None of these explanations offer any real insight into Sullivan's motivations, but all add to the folklore surrounding this event, thereby enhancing Elvis's image as a notorious rock 'n' roller.

Notorious or not, Elvis returned a hero to his hometown of Tupelo shortly after his first appearance on *The Ed Sullivan Show*. On September 26, 1956, he sang at the Mississippi-Alabama Fair and Dairy Show, which had been the site of his first public performance so many years before. As a frightened ten-year-old in 1945, Elvis had stood on a chair to sing "Old Shep" into the radio microphone; this time, the small stage could barely

contain the nation's most controversial performer as he rocked through two 45-minute shows. An estimated 12,000 residents from Tupelo and the surrounding area turned out to welcome home their native son, who had put their sleepy Southern town on the map. Local officials proclaimed September 26 as "Elvis Presley Day," and Elvis repaid their hospitality by donating his $10,000 fee to the city of Tupelo.

By the fall of 1956, Elvis had shaken Middle America out of the complacency so associated with that decade. The young singer had made a name for himself in almost every entertainment medium: He had toured across the country, sold millions of records, and had taken television by storm. Only one arena of popular expression remained for Elvis to conquer—the movies.

The first time independent movie producer Hal Wallis saw Elvis perform, he was convinced that Elvis was going to become a major star. A veteran of the movie business for 25 years, Wallis had a stellar reputation. He had worked as an executive producer at Warner Bros. for several years before forming Hal Wallis Productions in 1944. In early 1956, Wallis happened to catch Elvis's act on one of the *Stage Show* episodes. The electrifying effect Elvis had on the women in the studio audience spelled movie magic to the keen-eyed producer. Wasting no time, he called Colonel Parker the next morning to set up a screen test for the controversial young singer.

After seeing Elvis perform on *Stage Show*, veteran producer Hal Wallis knew he could turn the young singer into a movie star.

Parker was cool, playing Wallis like the experienced dealmaker he was, before casually replying that Elvis was planning to be on the coast soon, and perhaps a meeting could be arranged.

On April 1, 1956, Elvis took a screen test with respected character actor Frank Faylen. They performed a scene from N. Richard Nash's play *The Rainmaker*, which was soon to be made into a major movie. It may have been April Fools' Day, but Elvis's screen test was taken quite seriously. His screen presence was powerful enough for Wallis to arrange a three-picture deal. If starmaker Hal Wallis had confidence in Elvis as an actor, then Hollywood was willing to accept that the young singer was well on his way to motion picture stardom.

Elvis had always loved the movies. When he was in high school, he had ushered at Loew's State Theater in Memphis. Later in his life, when his superstar status prevented him from going out in public, Elvis often rented an entire theater just to watch one movie in peace. From the beginning of his career, Elvis had aspired to be a movie actor. When his sudden notoriety opened the door for this to happen, he was eager to do whatever he had to do to make a career in the movies. "Singers come and go," Elvis said, "but if you're a good actor, you can last a long time."

At this time, Wallis was working exclusively for Paramount Pictures, but that studio had no suitable script for Elvis when he signed his contract with Wallis. So Elvis was loaned to 20th Century-Fox for a Civil War drama called *The Reno Brothers*. His part in the movie was a secondary role, and both Robert Wagner and Jeffrey Hunter had originally

been considered for the part. It was the first and last film in which Elvis appeared that was not specifically designed as a vehicle for him.

The movie's theme song was taken from a Civil War ballad called "Aura Lee" and reworked as "Love Me Tender." Elvis released the song as a single, which became immensely popular and gained wide exposure after he sang it on *The Ed Sullivan Show*. Because the tune was such a hit, the name of the movie was changed to *Love Me Tender* before it opened in New York on November 16, 1956. The storyline follows the fortunes of a farm family after the Civil War. Elvis plays the youngest son, Clint Reno, who marries his eldest brother's girl. Everyone presumes that the brother has been killed in the war, but he

returns unexpectedly. The family is torn apart by the consequences of the marriage, and in the end, Clint is shot and killed.

The producers of *Love Me Tender* worried that Elvis's fans would have a negative reaction to the movie's ending. Elvis's real-life mother, Gladys, was said to be shocked by his on-screen death. No one knew if people would stay away from theaters once word got out that Elvis's character was going to die in the last few frames. In the movie's original ending, Mother Reno, played by Mildred Dunnock, rings the bell for dinner as the remaining Reno brothers come to supper. The pain and sadness on their faces indicate that Clint has gone to the Great Beyond. The end credits immediately follow this poignant but

Above left and above: Elvis's death scene in *Love Me Tender* upset not only his mother but also his fans.

Elvis and costar Richard Egan take direction from Robert Webb on the set of *Love Me Tender.*

downbeat scene. After the shooting of *Love Me Tender* was completed, Elvis was called back to make another ending for the movie. In this version, his character does indeed survive. However, the ending that was actually used in the final version of the film represents a compromise between the two. Clint Reno is killed, but Elvis's face is superimposed over the final scene as he sings "Love Me Tender." This version rings true to the original script, but fans are left with a more positive image of their idol.

Love Me Tender has only four musical numbers, but the song "Love Me Tender" was such a big hit for Elvis that no one seemed to notice how few songs were in the movie. Some people have claimed that Hal Wallis hinted that Elvis's faithful backup musicians, Scotty Moore, Bill Black, and D.J. Fontana, were not

welcome in Hollywood. Supposedly, he thought the trio was too unsophisticated to participate in a Hollywood recording session. A group called the Ken Darby Trio backed up Elvis in the soundtrack recording sessions, but this was not Wallis's decision. He had nothing to do with the production of *Love Me Tender* because it was released by Twentieth Century-Fox. The story about the musicians is either untrue, or it is about another Hollywood producer. In fact, Moore, Black, and Fontana appear in later movies that Elvis made for Wallis.

Elvis got along well with his costars, and he often deferred to their greater experience in making movies. Richard Egan, who played elder brother Vance Reno, said about Elvis: "That boy could charm the birds from the trees. He was so eager and humble, we went out of our way to help him." Years later, Egan would cross paths with Elvis once again. During Elvis's 1972 engagement in Las Vegas, Egan stood up and began an ovation for his former costar after the final number. Throughout the production of *Love Me Tender,* Elvis nursed a crush on costar Debra Paget, beginning a career-long habit of falling for his female costars. In this case, however, his attentions went unnoticed because Paget was not interested. A couple of years older than Elvis, Paget was dedicated to her career at this point. Her mother, who was often on the set, had big plans for Debra, none of which involved Elvis.

The reviews of Elvis's first screen performance were brutal, which was no surprise considering the criticism by the popular press before he turned to acting. A reviewer for *Time* magazine compared Elvis's performance at various times in the movie to a sausage, a Disney cartoon figure, and a corpse. A review in *Variety* was more to the point: "Appraising Presley as an actor, he ain't. Not that it makes any difference." But the critics' sarcasm fell on deaf ears. When a huge cut-out of Elvis as Clint Reno was unveiled atop a New York City theater to promote the movie, thousands of fans showed up to see Elvis larger than life.

The first movie Elvis made for Hal Wallis was *Loving You*. It was developed by Wallis and writer/director Hal Kanter specifically for the young star. Not only was this musical drama designed to showcase Elvis's best tal-

Elvis's second film, *Loving You*, was loosely based on his own experiences as a young singer.

ents, but the storyline was rather ingeniously based on his own life. *Loving You*, which was released by Paramount in July 1957, stars Elvis as an unknown but talented singer who has a totally new sound. His character, Deke Rivers, hails from the South, but he doesn't fit in with the country-music crowd. A ruthless music promoter, played by Lizabeth Scott, recognizes Deke's unique talent and exploits him as a fresh face who appeals to teenage audiences. The media misrepresents his appeal and brands him a dangerous hothead until Deke proves he has simply been misunderstood. The storyline and the well-written tunes tailored to Elvis's musical style were guaranteed to attract his fans. Contrary to popular belief, Elvis received his first on-screen kiss in *Loving You*, not in *Love Me Tender*. The honor went to a young actress named Jana Lund. She had a small role in the movie as a sexy, young fan of Deke Rivers who, unfortunately for Deke, has a jealous boyfriend.

To get the script as close as possible to real-life events, Wallis sent director Hal Kanter to Memphis to observe Elvis's act and lifestyle while he was on the road. Kanter was in Shreveport when Elvis gave one of his last performances on the *Louisiana Hayride*. Kanter's movie attempts to capture the excitement that Elvis generated in his audience during a concert. The performance scenes in *Loving You* were accurate down to the constant popping of flashbulbs, the hysterical screaming of the audience, and the almost unbearable tension that built up before Elvis appeared on stage. In an article Kanter later wrote for *Variety*, he referred to Elvis's posi-

Other titles considered for *Loving You* included *Lonesome Cowboy, Something for the Girls,* and *Running Wild*.

tion in this mass hysteria as "the eye of the hurricane." It was a position Elvis would hold for the rest of his life.

Kanter also managed to depict the unpleasant side of Elvis's fame in *Loving You*. Fans are shown swarming around Deke Rivers in the film, just as Elvis was often followed and mobbed after he achieved a certain level of fame. Fans infringe on Deke's personal life, making demands on his time and badgering him with selfish requests. Deke's fancy new automobile is covered with lipstick messages and phone numbers in the same way that Elvis's cars had sometimes been defaced by female fans desperate to get his attention.

Though Elvis did not date either of his costars—Dolores Hart or Lizabeth Scott—while making *Loving You*, he did go out with an actress who had a bit part in the movie. Elvis met pretty Yvonne Lime while on the set. Lime later appeared on several television shows, including *Father Knows Best* and *The Many Loves of Dobie Gillis*. Yvonne revealed what it was "really" like to date Elvis in the movie magazine *Modern Screen*. The article was just a publicity piece that attempted to present Elvis as a shining example of wholesome living. According to Yvonne, Elvis was the perfect gentleman, he was devoted to his mother, and he liked to sing religious songs at parties. His rock 'n' roll image, long hair, and sideburns were explained away in the article as nothing more than a case of nonconformity. With a logic only to be found in fanzines, Yvonne claimed that Elvis wore long hair and sideburns for the same reason that adults grew beards.

Top: Elvis's cars were often ruined by messages from fans, a fact incorporated into *Loving You*. **Bottom:** The film concluded happily.

Elvis asked Vernon and Gladys to join him in Hollywood for the filming of *Loving You*, because he had missed their company so much while making *Love Me Tender*. Hal Kanter arranged for Vernon and Gladys, along with some family friends, to make a cameo appearance near the end of the movie as members of a concert audience. After Gladys's death, Elvis refused to watch *Loving You* because it was such a painful reminder of his mother. In addition to his parents, Elvis's longtime backup musicians, Scotty Moore, Bill Black, and drummer D.J. Fontana, appeared in the movie as members of a country-western band. Even the Jordanaires, a vocal group that frequently sang background harmonies for Elvis, popped up in the movie for a brief appearance.

The soundtrack for *Loving You*, which was Elvis's third long-playing album for RCA, reached number one on some pop charts. This particular record also established a pattern in which songs from Elvis's latest film would be combined with tracks from recording sessions to make up an album. Elvis's films then served as elaborate promotions for his albums and vice versa. This was part of the Colonel's plan to get as much mileage from Elvis's movies as possible. One vehicle promoted the other for the maximum exposure of both.

Elvis as Deke Rivers, accompanied by the Jordanaires, pours everything he's got into the finale.

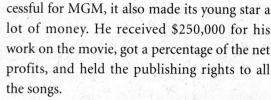

Less than four months later, Elvis's third feature film, *Jailhouse Rock*, opened the same day that the title song reached number one. This movie was not made by Hal Wallis's production company. Instead, Elvis had been loaned to MGM for this low-budget musical drama. Whereas *Loving You* was a polished feature film with glossy production numbers shot in candy-color Technicolor, *Jailhouse Rock* was a low-budget, straightforward black-and-white movie with simple back-lot sets and no large-scale production numbers. Far from bringing the movie down, these features enhance the gritty subject matter. *Jailhouse Rock* is generally regarded as the best movie Elvis ever made, even by present-day critics and historians who are not Presley fans. *Jailhouse Rock* was not only financially suc-

cessful for MGM, it also made its young star a lot of money. He received $250,000 for his work on the movie, got a percentage of the net profits, and held the publishing rights to all the songs.

In *Jailhouse Rock*, Elvis stars as Vince Everett, a hotheaded young man who becomes bitter after a stint in prison on a manslaughter charge. While he's in the pen, Vince learns to sing and play the guitar from another inmate who had once been a country-western performer. After his release from prison, Vince becomes a popular singer whose fresh sound creates a stir in the recording industry. With the help of a record promoter named Peggy Van Alden, who also falls in love with him, Vince enjoys popular success and critical acclaim. Once again, the plot echoes Elvis's own career, particularly when Vince is called to Hollywood because of his success as a singer.

Unlike *Loving You*, the movie *Jailhouse Rock* plays on the notorious side of Elvis's image. In this movie, he's a rebel. Elvis's character is not always likable. His bitterness over his unfair jail sentence is presented as a flaw in his character, but it allows a brooding, hot-blooded Elvis to explode on the screen. Not surprisingly, by the end of the movie, Vince has reformed into a nice guy who humbly wins the affections of Peggy Van Alden. But before he calms down, the audience is treated to several passionate scenes with provocative and often hip dialogue. During an argument between Peggy and Vince, Vince grabs Peggy and kisses her long and hard on the lips. Peggy acts as though she were appalled and haughtily

Above and below: In *Jailhouse Rock*, Mickey Shaughnessy costarred as the convict who teaches Elvis's character to play the guitar.

informs Vince that she doesn't appreciate his tactics. Vince coolly replies, "Them ain't tactics, honey, it's just the beast in me." It was a line guaranteed to send the women in the movie audience into a full-fledged swoon. Later in the film, a vacuous Hollywood starlet asks Vince what he thinks of her skimpy outfit. Vince's snappy comeback, "Flippy, really flippy," echoed the ultra-hip slang of a new generation.

Just as Elvis's fans were shocked to see their idol gunned down in *Love Me Tender*, so they were surprised to see Elvis's famous ducktail get clipped in *Jailhouse Rock*. As Vince enters prison, a regulation haircut is required. The prison barber hacks at Vince's hair, leaving the young man with the look of a freshly mowed lawn. Some biographers insist that Elvis wore a wig during the haircut scene.

Jailhouse Rock also contains several legendary production numbers, including the title tune, which was choreographed by Elvis himself. The number showcases Elvis's offbeat performing style, using a Hollywood musical format with background dancers and a stylized set. Elvis doesn't quite cut loose into his spontaneous gyrations during "Jailhouse Rock," but this musical sequence manages to capture the essence of his rebel image. Elvis, as Vince, also sings "Baby, I Don't Care" at a Hollywood pool party. All the partygoers are dressed in fashionable, light-colored swimwear except Elvis's character. He's dressed in black slacks and a black, long-sleeved sweater. Ironically, the partygoers look out of place; Elvis looks hip, not because of his clothes, but because of his attitude.

Elvis helped work out the choreography for the famous "Jailhouse Rock" production number.

Judy Tyler made her second and last big-screen appearance in *Jailhouse Rock*. She was killed shortly after shooting was completed.

Elvis did not date his leading lady, Judy Tyler, but he went out occasionally with Anne Neyland, who had a secondary role. Judy Tyler, who played Peggy Van Alden, had been a regular on the childrens television show *Howdy Doody*. She was Princess Summerfall Winterspring. Sadly, Tyler was killed in an auto accident after principal photography was completed. Her death made it difficult for Elvis to watch *Jailhouse Rock*. He did not attend the movie's preview in Hollywood, and he didn't appear at the premiere in Memphis in the fall of 1957.

Elvis's next movie, *King Creole*, was produced by Hal Wallis for Paramount. Based on Harold Robbins's novel *A Stone for Danny Fisher*, this musical drama stars Elvis as troubled teenager Danny Fisher. Dean Jagger costars as Danny's father, a man who has fallen apart emotionally since the death of his wife, letting his family slip into dire poverty. Determined to help his family regain the security and status it once had, Danny quits school to earn money by sweeping floors in a nightclub. A local mobster, played by Walter Matthau, takes an interest in Danny after he hears the talented young man sing. Danny becomes a regular performer in the mobster's club, packing in the crowds with his explosive performing style. But Danny seals his tragic fate when he becomes romantically involved with the mobster's girl.

Wallis had other intentions for this property when he first purchased it in 1955. At that time, a play version of *A Stone for Danny Fisher* was playing off-Broadway, and Wallis may have originally intended the title role to go to Ben Gazzara, with more of the novel left intact. Rumor has it that James Dean was also considered as a possibility for the role. When Wallis decided to use Elvis for the part of Danny Fisher, the original storyline had to be changed to accommodate Elvis's rock 'n' roll image. The setting was changed from New York City to New Orleans, although few characters other than Elvis speak with Southern accents. In the novel, Danny is an aspiring boxer; in the movie, he's an exciting young singer with a new sound.

Both Wallis and Paramount considered this movie to be an important project. The supporting cast features many notable actors including Carolyn Jones, Dean Jagger, and Walter Matthau, and the movie was directed by respected veteran Michael Curtiz, who made *Casablanca*, *Yankee Doodle Dandy*, *Angels with Dirty Faces*, and many other Hollywood classics. The high-quality production values plus the care taken in selecting the cast and crew paid off, because the movie earned Elvis his best movie reviews. Many

critics agreed that Elvis had improved tremendously as an actor, while others took note that he was "no longer depicted as the churlish, egotistical singing idol."

King Creole was shot in part on location in New Orleans. The film made effective use of such local sites as the French Quarter, Lake Pontchartrain, and a local high school. During location shooting, Elvis had a major problem with fans mobbing him at the Roosevelt Hotel, where he was staying. Hal Wallis arranged for heavy-duty security so that Elvis could get enough rest to look fresh on camera. Pinkerton guards patrolled the hallways, the elevators, and even the fire escapes of the hotel to keep well-intentioned but troublesome fans away. When he returned to his hotel in the evening, Elvis had to go to the top of an adjacent building, cross over the roof, and

Above: *King Creole* was considered a major Hollywood production. **Far left:** Director Michael Curtiz and producer Hal Wallis confer with Elvis behind the scenes. **Left:** Elvis, as Danny Fisher, scuffles with Vic Morrow's character, Shark.

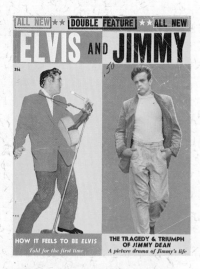

enter the Roosevelt by way of a fire escape. He was unable to enjoy New Orleans' celebrated nightclubs or famous restaurants because of the persistence of his fans. Shooting in the city's streets was even worse; city policemen had to be used for crowd control. By this time, Elvis Presley had entered that phase of his career that would keep him in seclusion, away from the fans who not only made him a star but also made him a recluse.

Elvis's first four movies are nothing like his later musical comedies. Aside from *Love Me Tender*, the plots of his early movies echo aspects of Elvis's image or actual events in his life. *Loving You* is a conventional Hollywood treatment of Elvis's rise to fame. *Jailhouse Rock* capitalized on Elvis's sensual, bad-boy image, and *King Creole* made use of certain details that paralleled Elvis's own life. In these movies, Elvis was clearly being groomed to take over for actor James Dean, who died in September 1955. Elvis appealed to teenage audiences in much the same way Dean and the young Marlon Brando had. An article in *Photoplay* magazine that was published during the shooting of *Love Me Tender* indicated that David Weisbart, the producer of Dean's best-known movie, *Rebel Without a Cause*, was talking to Elvis about portraying Dean in a movie biography. Elvis's role in *King Creole* had supposedly been offered to Dean. In 1956, a special single-issue magazine called *Elvis and Jimmy* showed how closely the two young men were linked in the popular imagination. The magazine designated Elvis to take up the fallen hero's leather jacket and become the premier teen rebel.

Elvis admired James Dean a great deal and must have been flattered by the comparisons to his hero. *Rebel Without a Cause* was one of Elvis's favorite movies. He memorized all the dialogue and recited Dean's lines whenever he got the chance. When Elvis went to Hollywood, he must have been eager to fill Dean's shoes, but he was humble: "I would never compare myself in any way to James Dean because James Dean was a genius. I sure would like to, I mean, I guess a lot of actors in Hollywood would like to have had the ability that James Dean had, but I would never compare myself to James Dean in any way." For a while, Elvis hung out with Dean's crowd, especially the young actor Nick Adams, and he dated Dean's *Rebel* costar Natalie Wood.

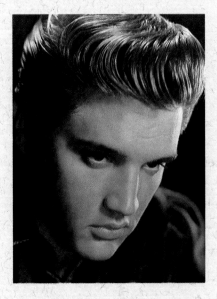

Above left and above: Did Colonel Parker's overall plan for Elvis's career hinder his future as a serious actor? Opinions vary; questions remain.

If Elvis had not gone into the army and returned home with a new image, would he have become the new Dean or another Brando? Many biographers and rock 'n' roll historians, who bemoan Elvis's later musical comedies, speculate that Elvis could have indeed been a good actor if it had not been for the Colonel. Elvis was considered for parts in such dramatic features as *The Rainmaker, The Way to the Gold*, and *The Defiant Ones*. He was also asked to appear in the musical comedy *The Girl Can't Help It*. The movie, starring Jayne Mansfield, was to feature the hottest rock 'n' roll stars of the day singing their biggest hits. Little Richard, Gene Vincent, and Eddie Cochran did appear in the movie. But, the Colonel told the producers that Elvis's fee would be a flat $50,000 for one song. The producers declined.

Colonel Parker's hardball tactics alienated some people in Hollywood, though he managed to secure lasting business relationships with many. His machinations, as well as the single-minded career course he had in mind for his "boy," are blamed for hindering Elvis's future as a serious actor. How true these accusations are remains open to debate. Few are left who can truly shed light on the validity of these claims against the Colonel. However, Hal Wallis, who negotiated with Colonel Parker many times, had this to say about the former carny: "I'd rather close a deal with the Devil."

CHAPTER FOUR

THIS IS THE ARMY

"DEAR PRIVATE PRESLEY: MY DADDY TELLS ME THE ARMY
IS GOING TO MAKE IT REAL HARD FOR YOU BECAUSE YOU
ARE FAMOUS....ARE THEY TREATING YOU BAD?
IF THEY ARE, I'LL FIX THEM GOOD."

—*Letter from fan Elinore Stevens, 1958*

Above and right: Elvis's ducktail haircut and style of clothing was emulated by teenagers but criticized by adults.

Elvis Presley's image as the notorious unruly rock 'n' roller dominated the publicity surrounding his career. He was Elvis the Pelvis, the boy with a snarl on his lips and the moves on his hips. It was a designation that Elvis hated, calling it "one of the most childish expressions I ever heard coming from an adult." This image originated from his unique singing and performing style—a style as alien to the adults north of the Mason-Dixon Line as it was unwelcome. After Elvis appeared on television and created a national controversy, many religious leaders, parents' organizations, and community leaders in the South also condemned the young singer and his music. Prior to his nation-wide exposure—when his image was that of a young country singer with a hot, new sound—Elvis had created only a mild stir in his native South.

In addition to his performing style, Elvis's hair and clothing were condemned as tasteless, and sometimes even vulgar. But it was the effect he had on his female audience that was considered the most alarming aspect of Elvis Presley. Teenage girls screamed uncontrollably through most of his performances. It seemed to those who didn't understand—critics, parents, teachers, community leaders, and religious groups—that Elvis inspired chaos and hysteria in young girls. Actually, Elvis controlled his audiences masterfully, manipulating their expectations and orchestrating their screaming for maximum effect. Rudy Vallee and Frank Sinatra had a similar effect on their audiences, but the obvious sensuality of Elvis's performing style made him seem more dangerous.

Elvis's movies helped recast this image somewhat. Three of the films, *Loving You*, *Jailhouse Rock*, and *King Creole* featured him in the role of an electrifying talent who had simply been misunderstood by the establishment. Basically sympathetic parts, the characters in these films helped mold his image into something more palatable to the public. Also, his financial success in all arenas of entertainment plus his ever-soaring popularity resulted in a more fitting nickname, the King of Rock 'n' Roll. The origins of his most famous title are not certain. May Mann, an entertainment columnist for many years, claimed to have used it first while others cite a *Variety* article from October of 1956 as the source.

Despite his success—and perhaps because of it—the mainstream press continued to criticize him at every turn. Reporters for nationally based magazines reinforced the notorious side to his image by harping on the antics of his fans, his greasy hair and sideburns, and his Beale Street attire.

Elvis's attire was always a major issue in the press. In 1956, his black slacks with a pink stripe running down the outside of the leg were cited as particularly tasteless. The following year, Elvis's gold lamé jacket drove reporters wild. Elvis asked the famed Hollywood clothing designer Nudie Cohen to create a special suit for him for his spring tour across the northern United States and parts of Canada. The suit consisted of a pair of gold slacks and a jacket woven from spun gold thread. Critics and journalists responded to Elvis in his gold suit like a bull to a red flag. Along each leg of the tour, newspapers never failed to mention the legendary gold tuxedo. As the tour progressed, the cost of the suit was reported as being higher and higher. According to the *St. Louis Post-Dispatch*, the

Bottom and left: Elvis's gold lamé suit was made by Nudie Cohen, who designed ostentatious clothing and gaudy automobiles for celebrities.

Above: Nudie Cohen poses with his famous client. **Below:** Elvis was always grateful for the support of his teenage fans.

suit cost Elvis $2,500; the *Fort Wayne News Sentinel* reported that the jacket alone had been $2,000; by the time he reached Canada, the price of the suit had jumped to $4,000. Though other entertainers, particularly Liberace, could wear outrageous costumes without criticism, Elvis was always ridiculed.

But it seemed Elvis wasn't allowed to do what other entertainers did without inviting attacks. Even his 1957 Christmas album created a furor. A standard Christmas album with fairly conventional arrangements of classic carols, *Elvis's Christmas Album*, was similar to the holiday fare offered by other singers. However, a radio station in Portland, Oregon, fired one of its disc jockeys because he played Elvis's "White Christmas" on the air. Management claimed the song was in bad taste. Dick Whittinghill of station KMPC of Los Angeles refused to play any songs from the album. He said that Elvis singing Christmas songs was "like having Tempest Storm [a stripper] give Christmas presents to [his] kids." Several radio stations in Canada

banned the album, while Chicago station WCFL banned all records by Elvis Presley.

The controversy generated by Elvis's image did nothing to deter the adulation of his teenage fans. By the same token, their outrageous loyalty did nothing to improve Elvis's relationship with the public as a whole. In 1956, Elvis said: "Teenagers are my life and my triumph. I'd be nowhere without them." But even he could not believe the lengths they would go to be near him. In Texas, his fans broke through the plate glass door of a theater to get close to him. In New Orleans, a group of girls tied up an elevator operator, captured Elvis, and held him prisoner inside the elevator. If his fans discovered Elvis's car in a parking lot during or after a concert, they would cover it with messages in lipstick. Fans broke into one of his Cadillacs and stole his collection of cigarette lighters. They also covered the exterior of the car with phone numbers etched into the paint with nail files or jewelry. Rumors circulated that fans were willing to have any body part autographed, and fan magazines warned girls to beware of Elvis's "doll-point pen." Some girls had their hair cut to look like Elvis's famous ducktail, complete with simulated sideburns.

In Memphis, fans often hung around his house, hoping to catch him at home. Sometimes he ventured outside and talked with them for hours at a time; sometimes Gladys served them refreshments on the patio. Initiates to the local Elvis Presley fan clubs were often seen picking blades of grass from the lawn as part of the requirement for membership. While the Presleys were living on Audubon Drive, their neighbors brought a law

suit against them for creating a public nuisance, but the magistrate ruled in favor of Elvis and his family. He maintained that the behavior of his fans was neither Elvis's fault nor his responsibility.

It soon became obvious that the house on Audubon Drive was woefully inadequate, not only because of the lawsuit but also because of the lack of privacy caused by overzealous fans. In March of 1957, Elvis purchased a large, 18-room home in the township of Whitehaven, which was mostly rolling countryside at that time. The house, christened Graceland by its previous owners, had been built in 1939 by Dr. Thomas Moore and his wife, Ruth. The estate was named in honor of Ruth Moore's aunt, Grace Toof. Elvis purchased the home, plus 14 acres of land for about $100,000.

Virginia Grant, the real estate agent who sold the property, has written a short memoir entitled *Exactly as It Happened: How Elvis Bought Graceland* in which she recounts the details of the sale. At first, Grant had looked for another ranch-style house for the Presleys, similar to the one on Audubon Drive, but when Gladys told her that Elvis wanted a large Colonial home, Grant realized she had been on the wrong track: "Without hesitation, and as if God himself put the thought in my mind and the words on my tongue, I immediately picked Graceland as the home for them, though I had never been in the house myself."

Located at what is now 3764 Elvis Presley Boulevard, Graceland is faced with pink Tennessee fieldstone and features a white-columned portico reminiscent of plantation houses in the antebellum South. Elvis spent an estimated $500,000 remodeling the house to

Top: Vernon, Elvis, and Gladys relax at their home on Audubon Drive. **Bottom:** Elvis's fleet of cars had increased by the time he lived on Audubon.

Left, below, and below left:
When Elvis purchased Graceland in 1957, the surrounding area was rolling countryside. Elvis purchased this country estate plus 14 acres of land to ensure some privacy.

suit his tastes and his family's needs. Eventually, the house was expanded to 23 rooms, including eight bathrooms. In addition to remodeling, an eight-foot high pink fieldstone fence was built around the property to help control the crowds of fans who had become accustomed to dropping by. The famous Music Gate was set into the fence at the bottom of the driveway facing the main road. Designed by Abe Saucer and custom-built by John Dillars, Sr., the wrought-iron gate features two guitar-wielding figures against a background of musical notes. Supposedly, the notes represent the opening bar of "Love Me Tender."

Shortly after moving into Graceland, Elvis looked out his window to discover a man picking leaves outside the stone fence and stuffing them into a briefcase. The Colonel and Elvis sauntered outside to investigate. Upon questioning the young man, they found

he planned to sell the leaves to fans in Buffalo, New York, for ten dollars apiece. The gimmick must have appealed to the Colonel's carny instincts because Parker let the man go. The Colonel even called a few local radio stations, suggesting they come out to Elvis's yard and rake his leaves, which could then be offered in various contests.

Despite the predominance of negative stories about Elvis in the press, another type of publicity began to emerge slowly but surely. This new pattern of publicity presented a different Elvis Presley—one that was contradictory to the high-profile figure who had caused so much controversy. This gentler side of his image has come to be known in the Elvis lore and literature as the "other Elvis" or the "good Elvis."

The "other Elvis" surfaced on July 1, 1956, on the television interview program *Hy Gardner Calling*. The program consisted of syndicated columnist Gardner calling one or two celebrities on the telephone each week. A split-screen technique allowed viewers to watch both Gardner and each celebrity talking on the phone. The episode featuring Elvis gave the young singer an opportunity to dispel some of the vicious rumors that were circulating about him, including one that purported he often smoked marijuana to reach the frenetic state necessary for his performing style and another that he had once shot his mother. Viewers saw a down-to-earth Elvis, who admitted that he was experiencing confusion over the enormity of his success. He also professed disbelief that critics could find his music to be a negative influence on anyone.

Stories about Elvis's close relationship with his parents began to appear in print. The

Below: At the gates of Graceland, Elvis signs some autographs. He would never quite find the privacy he was seeking. **Above:** Colonel Parker booked Elvis for several charity events, hoping to counter his client's rebel image.

fact that he didn't smoke or drink was brought out in some articles. Elvis was known to be polite during interviews, referring to his elders as "Sir" or "Ma'am." Colonel Parker publicized Elvis's strong feeling about helping less-fortunate people and booked him for many charity benefits, including those for the American Cancer Society and the March of Dimes.

Still, publications such as *Collier*'s magazine touted singer Pat Boone as a more clean-cut—and therefore more appropriate—teenage idol than Elvis Presley. Parker then tried to make Elvis seem more wholesome by getting his name and picture on a line of products. The Colonel sealed a deal with promoter extraordinaire Hank Saperstein to merchandise Elvis along the same lines as his other famous clients, who included Wyatt Earp, the Lone Ranger, and Lassie. Every kid in the country could find these all-American heroes on everything from lunchboxes to T-shirts. The Colonel wanted Elvis's likeness to be plastered on these kid-related items as well. In addition to the usual line of children's items, teenage girls were able to buy Elvis Presley lipstick in Hound Dog Orange, Tutti Frutti Red, and Heartbreak Hotel Pink. They could also hope for good luck from their Elvis Presley charm bracelets.

Aside from the added grist for the publicity mill generated by this side to Elvis's personality, the significance of the "other Elvis" lies in the Colonel's continual efforts to gain acceptance for the controversial singer with the mainstream audience. Parker exploited

Below: Elvis looks over some of the items that would bear his name and likeness after the Colonel signed a merchandizing deal with Hank Saperstein.
Below right: A fan dressed in Elvis finery waits for her idol to appear.

this aspect of Elvis's image to counter or balance the depiction of Elvis as a hedonistic rock 'n' roller, trying to push the singing idol closer and closer toward respectability.

But nothing that the Colonel or Elvis did to improve his image came close to generating the amount of positive publicity that Elvis gained after he was inducted into the army. Near the end of December 1957, Elvis received his draft notice, though he knew for some time that he might be drafted. Paramount, Elvis, and Hal Wallis requested a two-month deferment from the proposed January induction so that Elvis could finish shooting *King Creole*.

On March 24, 1958, Elvis was inducted into the U.S. Army, taking indoctrination at Fort Chaffee, Arkansas. A few days later, he was taken to Fort Hood, Texas, where he began basic training. Much publicity was generated from the events surrounding his induction, particularly the shearing of his famous hair. The Colonel, brandishing a 16mm movie camera, accompanied Elvis through the induction process, along with an entourage of reporters and photographers.

Elvis had refused to join the special services of the army as an entertainer, and he had turned down offers from the Marines and the Navy to enlist with them before he was drafted. Elvis's refusal to accept special consideration was seen by the public as admirable, particularly after Colonel Parker leaked to the press exactly how much money Elvis stood to lose by serving his country. Elvis wanted to be treated just like any other G.I., and he always insisted that once his fellow soldiers realized that he was there to pull his own weight, they would treat him like everyone else.

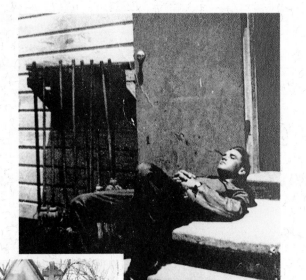

After basic training at Fort Hood, Elvis served two years in the Third Armored Division in West Germany. Although he was away from his fans and career, Elvis was not totally absent from the music scene. Parker and RCA made sure that Elvis had recorded enough material so that several records could be released while he was in the army. The movie *King Creole* did not open until several months after his induction, helping to keep Elvis before the public eye.

Five months after going into the army, Elvis suffered the tragedy of his mother's death. Gladys Presley died on August 14, 1958, possibly from a heart attack related to the acute hepatitis that had hospitalized her. Gladys was 46 when she died, although many accounts list her age at death as 42. (Gladys was embarrassed to be older than Vernon and

Right: Elvis took basic training at Ft. Hood in Texas. **Below left and below:** Gladys Presley died on August 14, 1958, and was buried at Forest Hill Cemetery in Memphis.

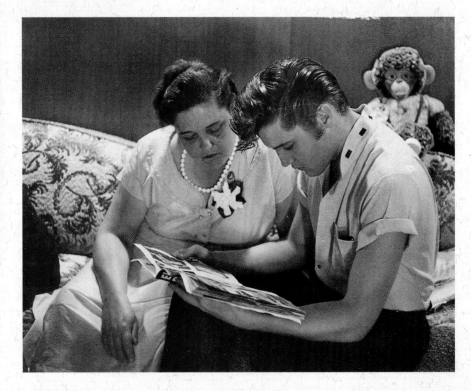

often said that she was four years younger than she actually was.) Elvis was devastated by his mother's death and broke down in front of reporters many times during the days before her funeral. The Blackwood Brothers gospel group sang Gladys's favorite hymns at the funeral, and many celebrities sent condolences, including Marlon Brando, Dean Martin, Ricky Nelson, Tennessee Ernie Ford, and Sammy Davis, Jr. Gladys was originally buried at Forest Hill Cemetery in Memphis, but after Elvis died, her remains were moved next to his at Graceland.

Shortly after his mother's funeral, Elvis was stationed in Bad Nauheim, West Germany, where he was allowed to live in a rented house near the base. He was joined by his father and grandmother. Elvis's German fans were as persistent as his fans in America. The Germans called Elvis their "rock 'n' roll matador." In Europe, the constant presence of fans and photographers made it difficult for Elvis to enjoy any tourist activities.

Near the end of his tour of duty, Presley met 14-year-old Priscilla Beaulieu through a mutual friend, U.S. Airman Currie Grant. She was in Germany because her stepfather, Air Force Captain Joseph Paul Beaulieu, was stationed in Wiesbaden. Priscilla's father had been killed in a plane crash when she was six months old, and Beaulieu adopted her shortly after he married her mother. Priscilla always referred to him simply as her father. Elvis had been stationed in Germany for some time before the Beaulieu family arrived. Priscilla told her dad that she hoped she'd run into Elvis, but he replied that he wouldn't let her walk across the street to see Elvis Presley!

Left and below: While stationed in Germany in Bad Nauheim, Elvis was allowed to live off base in a rented house with his father, grandmother, and a few friends.

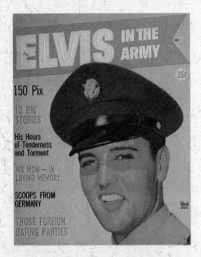

Above: Though Elvis was out of the music scene for two years, the fanzines still gave him ample coverage. **Right:** Elvis arrives at Ft. Dix in New Jersey for his discharge from the army.

Elvis and Priscilla dated frequently during his last few months in Germany, but their dates consisted of her visits to his rented home because of Elvis's inability to go out in public. Elvis liked to have a lot of people around him when he was home, so it's likely that when Priscilla visited him, several family members and friends were on hand as well. She was photographed by the press at the airport when Elvis left for America, and some of those photos ended up in *Life* magazine. In general, however, there was surprisingly little publicity about Elvis's interest in such a young girl.

When he got back to the states, Elvis downplayed questions about the girl he left behind. He may have done this to protect the Beaulieus from the press. Almost as soon as Elvis arrived home, gossip columnists began to link him romantically with Frank Sinatra's daughter, Nancy, although the relationship was probably not very significant for either one of them.

Priscilla visited Graceland many times over the next couple of years before Elvis asked her parents if they would let Priscilla stay in Memphis. In 1962, Elvis finally persuaded the Beaulieus to allow Priscilla to live with Vernon and finish school in Memphis. The press would have had a field day if this information had leaked out, but despite the fact that Priscilla lived with Elvis and his family during much of the time she was in high school, Elvis and Priscilla's private life remained private.

Elvis wasn't the only member of the Presley family to find romance in Germany.

While there, Vernon met Dee Stanley, who was in the process of divorcing her husband. In July 1960, shortly after Elvis's return to the States, Vernon and Dee were married in Huntsville, Alabama. Some people say that Vernon's second marriage caused friction between Elvis and his father, but it's impossible to say how much it affected their long-term relationship. At any rate, Elvis did not attend his father's wedding ceremony. Vernon and Dee's marriage ended in divorce in 1977.

While Elvis was in the service, critics speculated that the two years away from the public would seriously damage his career. His position at the forefront of rock 'n' roll was likely

Nancy Sinatra was on hand to greet Elvis after his army discharge and to offer him a present from her famous father.

to be lost. To some extent, they were correct. Elvis didn't return to the forefront of rock music when he came back from the army because he chose not to.

Elvis and Colonel Parker were no longer interested in rock 'n' roll, which had undergone many changes between 1958 and 1960. If anything, rock musicians were more controversial than ever: Little Richard was in trouble with the IRS and had abandoned rock 'n' roll for religious reasons; Chuck Berry had been arrested for violating the Mann Act; and Jerry Lee Lewis was ostracized for doing exactly what everyone thought Elvis would do. Lewis ran away with and married a 13-year-old girl. To make matters worse, at least in the eyes of the press, the girl was his cousin; and if that wasn't inflammatory enough, he was already married at the time. All of these scandals

served to temporarily put their careers on hold as well as to damage rock 'n' roll's already dubious reputation. While scandal claimed these rockers, others, including Buddy Holly and Ritchie Valens, fell victim to tragic deaths. The loss of these rock 'n' roll pioneers from the music scene contributed to the rise in popularity of ballad singers. As early as 1958, articles in music magazines began to note with pleasure that ballad singers were replacing the more frenzied performers on the charts.

When Elvis returned home in 1960, the stage was set for him to assume a more mellow style. The Colonel took advantage of the good publicity over Elvis's tour of duty to promote a mature Elvis Presley, who was being groomed to attract a mainstream audience. Rock 'n' roll fans and historians repeatedly view this change as a decline, but in reality, it was a deliberate change in Elvis's image. Elvis and the Colonel abandoned the notoriety of rock 'n' roll for the wider appeal of movies and pop music. In terms of financial success and overall popularity, they made the correct decision.

A single image sums up the ramifications of this important change in the young singer's career: Elvis's long, ducktail haircut—shorn amidst a whirl of publicity during his army induction—never grew back.

Below: Elvis changed his image and appearance after he got out of the army. His carefully groomed ducktail haircut and long sideburns never grew back. **Opposite page:** Elvis speaks at one of the many press conferences held after his army discharge.

CHAPTER FIVE

LEADING MAN

"HE'S THE BEST-MANNERED STAR IN HOLLYWOOD AND HE'S IMPROVED AS A PERFORMER AND HAS A DETERMINATION TO BE A FINE ACTOR. [ELVIS] WAS SMART ENOUGH TO SIMMER DOWN THAT TORRID ACT OF HIS."

—*Gossip columnist Hedda Hopper, early 1960s*

As soon as Elvis set foot on American soil after his discharge from the army, reporters descended on him with questions about his career. Newspaper interviews revealed that he did not intend to abandon rock 'n' roll "as long as people wanted it." Yet, almost immediately, Elvis and Colonel Parker embarked on a course designed to do just that. In doing so, they altered Elvis's image by using the same entertainment arenas that had constructed his image in the first place—recordings, television, and the movies.

Two weeks after his discharge, Elvis journeyed to Nashville for his first recording session in almost two years. Elvis was joined in the studio by two of his oldest friends, guitarist Scotty Moore and drummer D.J. Fontana. Bill Black, who had played doghouse bass for Elvis, was no longer part of his band. Moore, Black, and Fontana had been Elvis's backup musicians during most of his early career, but in the fall of 1957, Moore and Black resigned

Right and above: Elvis waits to board the bus he rented for the trip to Nashville to record *Elvis Is Back*, his first album released after his discharge from the army.

as regular members of Elvis's band. Money probably had a lot to do with their decision as Scotty and Bill were paid only $100 a week while they were in Memphis and $200 a week while they were on the road. It is assumed that the Colonel was responsible for the skimpy wages, though Elvis was never known to pay particularly high wages to any of the people who worked for him throughout his career. Black eventually formed his own group, Bill Black's Combo, and in 1959, they recorded an instrumental tune entitled "Smokie." Moore continued to record with Elvis in the studio on a free-lance basis until 1969. D.J. Fontana, who had been recruited from the *Louisiana Hayride*, had a separate arrangement with Elvis, which allowed him more leeway in his career.

Moore and Fontana were not the only musicians hired for the Nashville recording sessions. The famed country pianist Floyd Cramer signed on, and once again, the Jordanaires sang the backup vocals. During the first session, Elvis cut a single featuring "Stuck on You" on one side with "Fame and Fortune" on the flip side. In early April, Elvis returned to the RCA studio in Nashville to record the additional tracks that were needed to make an album. By the end of April, *Elvis Is Back* had been released. In less than two months, RCA had cut and pressed a brand-new Elvis Presley album, and it was playing on the radio.

Not all the songs that Elvis recorded in Nashville were included on the album *Elvis Is Back*. Two of his most acclaimed ballads, "It's Now or Never" and "Are You Lonesome Tonight?" were held back for later release.

During the sessions, Elvis also recorded a version of the song "Fever," which Peggy Lee had made famous two years earlier, and two rhythm-and-blues numbers, "Reconsider Baby" and "Such a Night." Elvis recorded his usual mix of rock, country, and rhythm-and-blues songs during these two April recording sessions, which yielded some of the best work of his career. Both "Are You Lonesome Tonight?" and "It's Now or Never" became number-one singles.

"Are You Lonesome Tonight?" was a clear departure from the kind of music that Elvis sang before he went into the army. In the 1920s, Al Jolson made this melancholy tune popular, but Elvis was probably more familiar with a 1959 version of the song that had been recorded by pop singer Jaye P. Morgan, who borrowed her arrangement from a 1950 rendition by the Blue Baron Orchestra. Colonel Parker is believed to have urged Elvis to record "Are You Lonesome Tonight" even though it was unusual for him to interfere with Elvis's choice of music. The song perfectly suited Elvis's new image as a mainstream pop singer.

"It's Now or Never" is based on the well-known Italian song "O Sole Mio." In 1949, Tony Martin recorded a pop-music version of "O Sole Mio," using English lyrics and the title "There's No Tomorrow." Elvis had heard Martin's rendition of the song, but he wanted new lyrics and a new arrangement of the tune before he was willing to record it. The new version was titled "It's Now or Never," and it became one of Elvis's signature songs. During 1960, Elvis recorded another song that was based on an Italian tune. "Surrender," a mod-

ern version of "Come Back to Sorrento," had been recorded by Dean Martin, who was supposedly Elvis's favorite pop singer. Because "Surrender" is only one minute and 51 seconds long, it has the distinction of being one of the shortest songs ever to reach number one on the pop charts.

On May 8, 1960, Elvis appeared on television for the first time since his discharge from the army. He was a guest on *The Frank Sinatra-Timex Special*, also known as *Welcome Home Elvis*. Colonel Parker made the deal with the show's producers months before

Above and left: Elvis's appearance on Frank Sinatra's television variety special in 1960 helped sell him to a mainstream audience.

Elvis was released from active duty. He hoped that appearing with Sinatra would introduce Elvis as a pop singer to a wide audience that would be made up of adults and pop enthusiasts as well as teenagers and country-western fans. Never one to take chances, the Colonel made sure that Elvis would make a big splash by packing the studio audience with 400 members of one of Elvis's biggest fan clubs. The program received phenomenal ratings, giving ABC-TV a 41.5 share for that evening. Elvis was paid a staggering $125,000 for a total of six minutes on the air.

Sammy Davis, Jr., Peter Lawford, and Joey Bishop also appeared on the television special. In addition to these members of Sinatra's famed "Rat Pack," the cast included Sinatra's daughter Nancy, whom the gossip columns had recently linked with Elvis. Elvis sang his two latest hits, and then later in the show, joined Sinatra for a short duet. Dressed in a conservative but stylish tuxedo, the former teen idol sang Sinatra's "Witchcraft," while Sinatra crooned Elvis's "Love Me Tender." His choice of clothes, his shorter hairstyle, and his connections with the Rat Pack indicated that Elvis's career was taking a new direction. When Elvis and Sinatra sang each other's songs, it was as though Sinatra was passing on his position as pop idol to the next generation. The Voice, as Sinatra was known in the 1940s, was making way for the King.

In Ed Sullivan's syndicated newspaper column, the crusty show business luminary spoke harshly of Elvis's appearance on the *Frank Sinatra-Timex Special*. Lingering bitterness over his dealings with Colonel Parker crept into his account of Elvis's appearance. Sullivan blasted Parker for allowing Elvis to sing only two songs in the special, stating, "Col. Tom, using the logic of a farmer, is a firm believer in not giving a hungry horse a bale of hay." Sullivan seemed to forget that it was Sinatra's special, not Elvis's, and that there were four other guests to showcase. Some jabs at Elvis's personal appearance rounded out the column as Sullivan noted the young singer, "minus his sideburns, has substituted what the ladies probably would call a 'high hair-do.' His hair is so high in front that it looks like a ski jump."

On March 25, 1961, Elvis performed live at the Bloch Arena in Pearl Harbor, Hawaii, at a benefit for the fund to build a memorial for the USS *Arizona*, which had been sunk on Pearl Harbor Day. Ticket prices for this performance ranged from three dollars to ten

Right: Colonel Parker decided to broaden Elvis's audience by turning him into a pop singer and movie star. **Opposite page:** In 1961, Elvis performed at a benefit to raise money for a memorial for the USS *Arizona*.

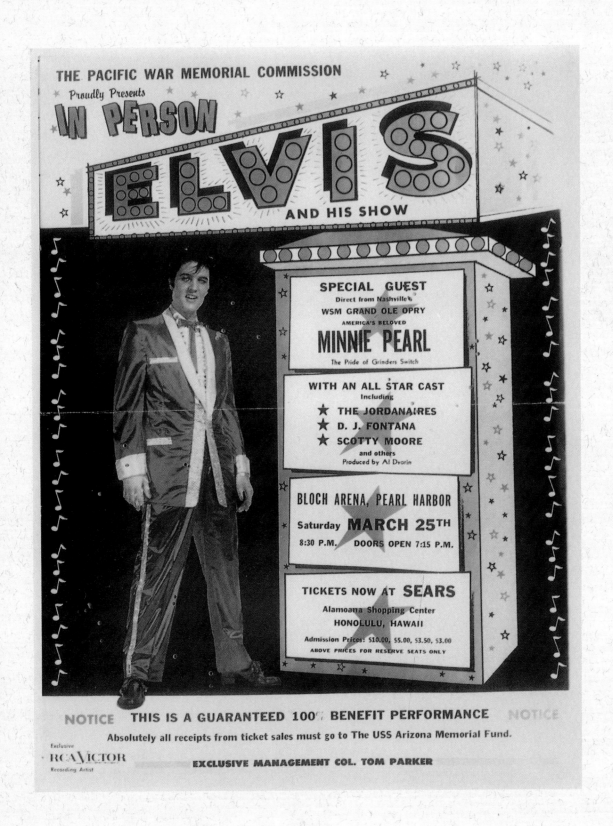

dollars, with 100 ringside seats reserved for people who donated $100. Elvis and Colonel Parker bought fifty special seats and donated them to patients from Tripler Hospital in Hawaii. Elvis's benefit raised more than $52,000 for the memorial fund. On March 30, the Hawaii House of Representatives passed Special Resolution 105 thanking Elvis and the Colonel.

Though the benefit for the *Arizona* memorial could be considered a good career move in that it helped Elvis become more acceptable to an adult audience, his career was not the only reason Elvis agreed to the benefit. He had a sensitive, generous nature, and throughout his entire life, Elvis gave freely to charities and other worthy causes, whether he received publicity for it or not. Five years after this benefit concert, while he was in Hawaii filming *Paradise, Hawaiian Style*, Elvis visited the completed memorial and placed a wreath. Photographers and reporters rushed in to record the event, but Elvis sent them away. He did not want his visit to the memorial to become a publicity stunt.

After the 1961 concert in Hawaii, Elvis did not give another live performance until 1969, and he made no television appearances after the Sinatra special until December 1968. Throughout most of the 1960s, if fans wanted to see Elvis, they had to go to the movies.

In May of 1960, Elvis returned to Hollywood to begin shooting *G.I. Blues*. The movie's storyline concerns a singer who is serving in the army in Germany. Producer Hal Wallis borrowed details from Elvis's own life to flesh out the script just as he had done in the two previous films he had made with Elvis. In *G.I. Blues*, Elvis's character is not only stationed in Germany, but he's also a member of a tank division just as Elvis had been.

G.I. Blues was the third and final movie Elvis made under his original contract with Hal Wallis. However, as soon as Elvis returned to Hollywood, Colonel Parker began to negotiate another three-picture deal with Wallis. Why Parker chose to tie Elvis down with multipicture contracts instead of negotiating on a film-by-film basis, which probably would have netted both Elvis and the Colonel more money, is not known. Still, Elvis received a handsome salary and a percentage of the profits in most of his contracts. At one point during the 1960s, he was the highest-paid actor in

Elvis's character in *G.I. Blues* served in the army in Germany in a tank division just as Elvis had done.

Hollywood. Parker also did well for himself through his practice of complicating standard contracts with side deals and promotions. He also received a screen credit for each of Elvis's 31 narrative features, most often as technical adviser.

Like the movies Elvis made before he went in the army, *G.I. Blues* is based on the events of his own life, but unlike those early efforts, *G.I. Blues* is a musical comedy instead of a musical drama. The movie is aimed at a family audience, and Elvis's controversial performing style has been toned down. He still moves freely when he sings, but he no longer swings his hips or swivels his leg in a sensual manner. Instead, several long-legged female dancers do it for him. Elvis's character has also changed; he's older, and his army uniform suggests maturity and responsibility. Even though most of the songs in *G.I. Blues* are fast-paced, they don't have the same hard-driving sound, sexual connotation, or emotional delivery that Elvis's early soundtrack recordings had. Elvis's screen image has been deliberately softened for *G.I. Blues*. In one scene, he sings a Bavarian-sounding folk tune during a children's puppet show, while in another, he baby-sits an adorable infant. The ads for *G.I. Blues* sum up these changes perfectly: "See and Hear the New Elvis: The Idol of the Teenagers is the Idol of the *Family* [author's emphasis]."

Elvis's hair is relatively short in the film compared to his wild ducktail haircut from the previous decade. His hair is also a different color. After the movie *Loving You* was released, Elvis began to dye his hair jet black, which had been the color of his mother's hair. Elvis's natural hair color was dark blond or light brown,

Above and left: Elvis's female costars in *G.I. Blues* were Sigrid Maier (IN OLIVE JUMPER) , Leticia Roman (IN RED DRESS), and Juliet Prowse (IN STRIPED DRESS).

though it usually looked darker because of the pomade that Elvis used to grease down his flamboyant ducktail. The two movies that Elvis made after *Loving You* were filmed in black and white, so the change in his hair color wasn't obvious. *G.I. Blues* and most of the other movies he made during the 1960s were shot in color, and the rich tones of Elvis's blue-black hair are quite noticeable.

In *G.I. Blues*, Robert Ivers and James Douglas play Elvis's closest friends, who just happen to be members of his band. In many of Elvis's movies, he has two or three buddies who are also his musicians. These movie sidekicks had their real-life counterparts in the form of Elvis's entourage of buddy body-

guards. Dubbed the "Memphis Mafia" by the press, these buddies accompanied Elvis wherever he went.

G.I. Blues was enormously successful; it ranked fourteenth in box-office receipts for 1960. The soundtrack album reached number one quickly, remaining on the charts longer than any other Elvis Presley album. Movie critics applauded the new Elvis. They approved of his new image and predicted he would find plenty of new fans among older women. Elvis didn't share the critics' enthusiasm for *G.I. Blues*. He felt that there were too many musical numbers, and he believed that some of them made no sense within the context of the plot. He was concerned that the quality of many of these songs was not as good as the music for his earlier movies.

Elvis was also eager to move on to more demanding and serious roles. The western *Flaming Star* gave Elvis the chance to prove himself as an actor. The movie brought together some of Hollywood's most notable actors and creative personnel. In this tense drama, Elvis was able to hold his own with veteran performers John McIntire and Dolores Del Rio. Newcomer Barbara Eden, who later starred in the television series *I Dream of Jeannie*, was also featured in the film. Director Don Siegel, who later won critical acclaim for his work on the original *Dirty Harry*, fashioned a strong statement on racial prejudice out of the script, which had been based on a popular novel by Clair Huffaker. Nunnally Johnson, a long-time Hollywood producer and screenwriter, cowrote the script with Huffaker. Established composer Cyril Mockridge produced the background music.

Because of California's child labor laws, three sets of twins played the role of Tiger, the baby in *G.I. Blues*.

In *Flaming Star*, Elvis plays the son of a white settler and a Kiowa Indian. His character has the unlikely but romantic name of Pacer Burton. A Kiowa uprising forces Pacer to choose sides between the white settlers and his mother's tribe. In addition to the central conflict, the movie presents the day-to-day prejudice Pacer experiences because of his half-caste status, which can be taken as a veiled reference to the problems African-Americans experienced during their struggle for civil rights in the 1950s and 1960s.

Stories have always circulated that the role of Pacer Burton was originally written for Marlon Brando, which seems to lend credence

Above left: Dolores Del Rio played Elvis's Native American mother in *Flaming Star*. It was her first Hollywood film in 18 years. **Above:** Native American stuntman Rodd Redwing taught Elvis to handle his pistol correctly.

to the speculation that Elvis could have or should have followed in Brando's footsteps. Yet, an accurate accounting of the sequence of events that lead to the production of *Flaming Star* reveals that it was merely coincidence that Brando and Elvis were considered for the same role. It took more than two years of negotiations and false starts for *Flaming Star* to get to the screen. In 1958, Twentieth Century-Fox bought the rights to Clair Huffaker's novel before it was completed. The novel was titled *The Brothers of Flaming Arrow* and focused on two characters. Marlon Brando and Frank Sinatra were offered the roles of the two brothers, but negotiations with the two stars broke down before the novel was finished. The title was changed to *Flaming Lance* when Huffaker finally completed writing. The focus of the plot was shifted to one character by Johnson and Huffaker at some point during the scriptwriting stage, and Elvis was offered the role of Pacer Burton in 1960. The project went through several title changes, including *Flaming Heart*, *Black Star*, and *Black Heart*, before *Flaming Star* was chosen. Hollywood productions frequently go through many stages, changing focus and casts at every turn. This was certainly the case with *Flaming Star*.

Despite the participation of such industry greats as Del Rio, Johnson, and Mockridge, *Flaming Star* was not considered a major success. Elvis's fans were disappointed because they expected Elvis to perform several songs, when he actually sang only two. A four-song print had been shown to a preview audience, but it was never released, perhaps because director Siegel thought that too many songs

detracted from the movie's serious tone. Though *Flaming Star* garnered favorable reviews, it was a box-office disappointment compared to *G.I. Blues*. *Flaming Star* was released near the closing days of December 1960 to coincide with the school holidays at Christmas, setting a pattern for the release of future Elvis Presley movies.

Elvis got one more shot at serious acting when he was signed to star in the drama *Wild in the Country*. The film was directed by Philip Dunne from a script by playwright Clifford Odets. *Wild in the Country* features Elvis as a young hothead from the rural South named Glenn Tyler, who tries to straighten out his life after serving time in a juvenile hall. He becomes romantically involved with three women, each representing some facet of his life. Tuesday Weld plays an uneducated country girl with an illegitimate child who urges Tyler to stay with his own kind. Hope Lange costars as a psychiatric consultant who encourages Tyler to go to college to pursue a writing career. When Lange's character falls in love with her client, she causes a local scandal. Millie Perkins plays Tyler's childhood sweetheart, who puts his interests ahead of her own, encouraging him to get an education even if it means giving her up. The three women represent Glenn's past, present, and future. Of the three actresses, Elvis's smoldering on-screen presence best complemented Tuesday Weld's sensual performance. Elvis and Weld grew close during the production of *Wild in the Country* and remained friends for several years.

No songs were included in the original script for this movie, but after the poor show-

Elvis enjoyed working with his three female costars in *Wild in the Country*: Hope Lange (LEFT), Tueday Weld (BELOW LEFT), and Millie Perkins (BELOW). In 1990, Perkins was cast as Elvis's mother, Gladys, in the short-lived television series *Elvis*.

Norman Taurog, the director of *Blue Hawaii,* instructs Elvis before rolling the camera.

ed to Elvis and the Colonel exactly what type of film Elvis's most devoted fans wanted to see him in. Elvis did not accept another serious role until the end of his film career.

Elvis returned to musical comedies with *Blue Hawaii,* one of his most commercially successful features. In playing Chad Gates, the son of a wealthy pineapple-plantation owner, Elvis discovered that the role bore little resemblance to those he had played in the past. Angela Lansbury costarred as Elvis's mother (despite being only 35 years old), a Southern belle from a wealthy, established family with political clout. The plot concerns the reluctance of easy-going Chad to trade in his Hawaiian shirt for a business suit. Pressured by his parents to join his father in running the plantation, Chad chooses to play music on the beach with his native Hawaiian friends.

Blue Hawaii was directed by Norman Taurog and features gorgeous Hawaiian scenery shot by cinematographer Charles Lang, Jr. Scenes were shot at Waikiki Beach, Hanauma Bay, and Ala Moana Park. In response to the fans' cry for more songs, *Blue Hawaii* contains 14 musical numbers, including the title song and one of Elvis's biggest hits, "Can't Help Falling in Love with You." The film includes a wide range of musical styles from the swinging "Rock-a-Hula Baby" to the comical "Ito Eats."

Director Taurog was a competent Hollywood craftsman whose best-known effort is the 1938 classic *Boys Town.* He worked on nine of Elvis's features—more than any other director. The mild-mannered Taurog was supposedly Elvis's favorite director because he was so sensitive to the needs of his star.

ing *Flaming Star* made at the box office, six musical numbers were added to *Wild in the Country.* Only four of them made the final cut. In addition to the title tune that is sung over the opening credits, Elvis sings a song to each of the three women in the movie. Even with the musical numbers, *Wild in the Country* was deemed a disappointment by Elvis's fans. Like *Flaming Star,* the movie didn't lose money at the box office, but it wasn't a smash success either. Both Elvis and Tuesday Weld were voted the Damp Raincoat Award as the most disappointing performers of 1961 by *Teen* magazine. While "awards" such as this would hardly ruin anyone's career, they indicat-

During the filming of *Blue Hawaii*, Elvis let it be known that he became nervous in deep water. Many scenes in the movie were scheduled to be shot in or near the ocean, and director Taurog sensed Elvis's apprehension. He gave the young actor the option of playing the scenes in the water, as called for in the script, or playing them on the beach. Elvis appreciated Taurog's sensitivity toward his problem and worked to overcome it. Eventually, he was able to get over his fear, and all the required scenes were shot with Elvis actually in the ocean.

While Elvis was trying to be cooperative, the Colonel seemed to be trying equally hard to be disagreeable. One rainy day when Taurog had waited for many hours for a break in the weather, the Colonel alienated almost everyone on the set with an inexplicable power play. Just as the rain finally stopped and Taurog rolled the cameras on a shot of Elvis running out of the surf, Parker rushed in front of the camera, calling, "Cut, cut." This was a violation of proper etiquette on a movie set, where no one stops a scene except the director. Producer Hal Wallis and director Taurog were furious and demanded to know what problem could possibly be important enough to cause Parker to stop the shot. Parker slyly pointed out that Elvis was wearing his own watch during the scene. The terms of his contract spelled out that Elvis was to provide no part of his wardrobe, including jewelry. If Wallis and Taurog wanted to use the take that had just been shot, they would have to pay Elvis $25,000 for providing his own wardrobe. Needless to say, Taurog had Elvis remove his watch, and the scene was reshot.

Blue Hawaii was released during the Thanksgiving-Christmas holidays in 1961, grossing almost five million dollars. The soundtrack album was the fastest-selling album of that year. Unfortunately for Elvis, the success of *Blue Hawaii* restricted him to acting in musical comedies. The Colonel, Hal Wallis, and the other members of his management team used the tremendous box-office figures to convince Elvis that this was the type of film his fans preferred.

The standard interpretation of Elvis's film career is to view this juncture as the beginning of the end, because he seemed to give up his dream of becoming a serious actor. But, Elvis made 23 movies after *Blue Hawaii*, all of which were financial and popular successes. It seems appropriate to give Elvis's film career a different spin: Though Elvis Presley failed to become a serious actor, he was an extremely successful movie star.

Below left: Elvis and a bevy of background dancers perform "Slicin' Sand." **Below:** *Blue Hawaii* was written to showcase some of the Islands' beautiful scenery.

Above: In *Blue Hawaii*, Jennie Maxwell played a precocious teenager with a crush on Elvis's character. **Above right and opposite page:** Joan Blackman costarred as Elvis's love interest. **Below:** Elvis and his beach buddies sing "No More."

Juliet Prowse was originally cast to play Maile Duval in *Blue Hawaii,* but the deal fell through, and Joan Blackman got the part.

Blue Hawaii was Elvis's highest-grossing film at the time of release. The success of this musical comedy helped convince Elvis that this was the type of film fans wanted to see him in.

CHAPTER SIX

THE PRESLEY TRAVELOGUES

Q: "WHAT KIND OF PART DO YOU PLAY IN *SPEEDWAY?*"

ELVIS: "I'M KINDUVA SINGIN' MILLIONAIRE-PLAYBOY-RACE DRIVER, SIR."

Q: "HAVE YOU EVER ASSAYED SUCH A PART BEFORE?"

ELVIS: "ONLY ABOUT 25 TIMES, SIR."

—Interview with Elvis, 1968

Above: Elvis's managment team included Colonel Tom Parker, producer Hal Wallis, and Abe Lastfogel of the William Morris Agency. **Opposite page:** The typical Elvis character was a boat pilot, race-car driver, or airplane pilot who could also sing!

No group of American films has been more ridiculed than Elvis Presley's musical comedies, which have been written off as mindless, unrealistic, formulaic, and trite. Much of the reasoning behind this view of his movies originated with Elvis himself. He was disappointed in his film career and disillusioned with Hollywood, an attitude revealed through some of the anecdotes from this period. During the production of one film, he quipped, "Hey, there are some pretty funny things in this script. I'm gonna have to read it someday." On another occasion, he confessed, "I'm tired of playing a guy who would be in a fight and would start singing to the guy he was beating up." Later, in press conferences and on stage, he routinely scorned his movies, poking fun at the type of character he played time and time again.

Many have echoed Elvis's negative opinion of his movies. The logic seems to be that if Elvis was ultimately disappointed in his film career then his films must be worthless. Some blame his film career for directing him away from rock 'n' roll, thereby leading him astray. Others point to the formulaic plots of his musical comedies as evidence that his film career declined after he was discharged from the army. Yet, no Presley picture ever lost money, and through the benefit of video and cable television, audiences still enjoy his 31 features. Elvis may have grown bitter over his Hollywood career for a variety of reasons, but his fans still respond with enthusiasm to his films. Elvis's personal feelings notwithstanding, the popularity of his films forces a re-evaluation of his acting career.

After the success of *Blue Hawaii* in 1961, Elvis's management team—producer Hal Wallis, Colonel Parker, and Abe Lastfogel of the William Morris Agency—convinced him that fans preferred him in lightweight musical vehicles. They felt that this film was a success because it had just the right mix of music, romance, and comedy. *Blue Hawaii* contained the formula on which most of Elvis's subsequent films were based. The typical Presley picture was a romantic musical comedy set in an exotic location, such as Mexico or Hawaii, or a well-known vacation spot, such as Las Vegas, Fort Lauderdale, or the Seattle World's Fair. Elvis played a fun-loving ski instructor, boat captain, pilot, or race-car driver who could also sing.

A Presley picture was usually packed with songs, averaging one every 12 to 13 minutes. In most of Elvis's pre-army films, the songs are performed almost entirely on a stage setting because his characters are up-and-coming singers. After *Blue Hawaii*, the stage settings were abandoned as his characters were rarely performers by occupation, resulting in the integration of the musical numbers into the storyline. In other words, Elvis's character would burst into song on a moment's notice, whether he happened to be on a boat, in a car, on the beach, or even on an amusement park ride. Though this had been standard practice in Hollywood musicals for years, Elvis found the tendency of his characters to break into song at any time to be foolish.

The sensuality that had marked Elvis's performing style in the previous decade disappeared in his musical comedies, because his

Opposite page: A Presley picture was often set in an exotic locale or at a vacation resort. Exteriors for *Girls, Girls, Girls* were shot in Hawaii. **Left:** Elvis's later musical vehicles were geared to family audiences and often included sentimental scenes with small children. Here, Elvis serenades Vicky Tiu in *It Happened at the World's Fair.*

character sometimes sang to a love interest or a child, making that style of performing inappropriate. Or, more often than not, Elvis was surrounded by a bevy of bathing beauties. Instead of Elvis swinging his hips provocatively, a group of female dancers did it for him.

With some notable exceptions, this formula defines the bulk of his movies, which Elvis disparagingly called "Presley travelogues." Film reviewers and Presley biographers refer to these movies as vehicles. In Hollywood, a vehicle is a film constructed around a star's image. In other words, a star plays a character based on their own personality rather than portraying a complex, three-dimensional character. Vehicles provide a showcase for performers to do their specialty, and, in this regard, musical stars tend to bene-

fit more than other actors from appearing in vehicles. Many well-respected musical and comedy stars have been showcased in vehicles, including Fred Astaire, Ginger Rogers, and Bob Hope. In this context, Hal Wallis's decision to display the talents of Elvis Presley in a series of musical comedies was a logical one.

Elvis was not the only pop-rock star to appear in a series of lightweight musicals during the 1960s. Everyone from Frankie Avalon to Herman's Hermits bopped through their own musical vehicles, which were marketed to youthful audiences. Some of these teen musicals featured pop-flavored songs that sounded more like some Hollywood executive's idea of what rock music should be, while others included the music of well-known rock 'n' roll bands of the era.

The most famous "teen flicks" included the series of beach movies produced by American International Pictures starring Frankie Avalon and Annette Funicello. The first, *Beach Party*, was released in 1963 and was so successful that it launched four others with the same cast—*Muscle Beach Party, Bikini Beach, Beach Blanket Bingo,* and *How to Stuff a Wild Bikini.* In each film, Funicello played DeeDee, who spent most of the plot trying to keep Frankie, played by Avalon, in check. A whole gang of stock players supported Frankie and Annette in their youthful shenanigans, including dancer Candy Johnson, whose deadly wiggle literally knocked men for a loop; John Ashley, who was often Frankie's rival for DeeDee's affections; and, Jody McCrae, a surf bum named Deadhead who had taken one too many spills.

Though their low-budget origins are apparent, the films captured the pleasures of youthful pastimes and the spirit of surfing music so popular during the early 1960s. Several bands known for the "surfin' sound" made guest appearances in the beach party movies, including Dick Dale and the Del-Tones, the Hondells, the Pyramids, and the Kingsmen. In addition, such well-known film actors from past generations as Robert Cummings, Buster Keaton, Dorothy Malone, Mickey Rooney, and Keenan Wynn rounded out the casts, lending this series an aura of legitimacy lacking in other teen flicks.

When the beach began to look a bit too familiar, the party moved to the ski slopes. A whole new subgenre was born after producer Gene Corman at American International decided to use a ski resort for the setting of *Ski*

Above and right: *Beach Party,* starring Frankie Avalon and Annette Funicello, was part of the youth-targeted genre known as teen flicks. Elvis's musical vehicles from the 1960s were also a part of this genre.

Party. Frankie Avalon courted Deborah Walley this time out while Dwayne Hickman was paired with Yvonne Craig. Leslie Gore and her pop-flavored songs fit right into the fluffy storyline, but James Brown's highly charged soul numbers burned through the screen when he boogalooed into the scene with his Famous Flames. Still other musicals made use of a college setting in an effort to keep this youth-oriented genre alive, including *Get Yourself a College Girl*, with Nancy Sinatra, Mary Ann Mobley, and Chad Everett, and *C'mon Let's Live a Little* with Bobby Vee and Jackie DeShannon.

Some of the English rock groups who were part of the British Invasion were also packaged into movie vehicles. Peter Noone and Herman's Hermits made a splash with their feature musical called *Hold On*, while the Dave Clark Five weren't quite up to par in a dismal effort titled *Having a Wild Weekend*.

The Beatles' two feature films, *A Hard Day's Night* and *Help!* belong to this musical genre as well, but the creative direction by Richard Lester lifts them above the exploitative level of the typical teen flick.

Most of the movies that starred pop-rock singers were meant strictly for teen audiences, but Elvis's musical comedies are family fare. The casts include children as well as older characters who are accepted as wise representatives of past generations. Despite these differences, Elvis's movies fit quite well into the teen musical genre. Many of Elvis's costars, for example, were featured in the beach and ski movies, including Shelley Fabares, Nancy Sinatra, Yvonne Craig, Deborah Walley, Joby Baker, Dwayne Hickman, and Mary Ann Mobley. Producers and directors from other teen musicals also worked on Elvis's films. Sam Katzman, the "King of the Quickies," who produced *Get Yourself a College Girl*, had been

Below left and below: The Beatles' feature films, *A Hard Day's Night* and *Help!*, represent more creative examples of teen flicks. Both were directed by the talented Richard Lester.

The beach and resort settings of Elvis's films parallel those of other teen flicks. **Above:** *Where the Boys Are* helped make the beach a popular setting. **Below:** Palm Springs proved a hot spot in *Palm Springs Weekend*. **Below right:** When European discotheques were all the rage, Elvis starred in *Double Trouble*.

in the youth exploitation market since he made some of the first rock 'n' roll vehicles during the 1950s. He was responsible for two of Elvis's films, *Kissin' Cousins* and *Harum Scarum*.

The settings and plots of Elvis's films parallel those of other youth-related musicals. When Easter vacation in Fort Lauderdale and other resort areas became a popular subject, as in *Where the Boys Are* and *Palm Springs Weekend*, Elvis starred in his own Lauderdale adventure called *Girl Happy*. When the mod scene in England and Europe was all the rage, Elvis appeared in *Double Trouble*, which featured the swinging discotheques of London and Amsterdam as a backdrop. The considerable number of beach-related films that Elvis made, including *Blue Hawaii*, *Clambake*, and *Paradise, Hawaiian Style*, was undoubtedly

influenced by the popularity of the beach party movies.

Placed within the context of the teen musical, Elvis's movies make perfect sense, even standing out because of the high-quality production values. A critic for *Variety* praised Elvis's movies for this reason in a review of *Easy Come, Easy Go*: "Anyone who has seen similar films recognizes the superior quality of Presley's films: the story makes sense; the songs are better, and better motivated; cast and direction are stronger; production values are first-rate." The teen musical genre, including Elvis's musical vehicles, is a testament to the popularity of that easy-going, pop-rock music of the mid-1960s and to those teen idols who were part of that scene. Never meant to be serious filmmaking, all of these films are best taken as lighthearted Americana.

Elvis returned to Hawaii for *Paradise, Hawaiian Style*. The location shooting for some of his films reflected the better production values of his movies compared to those of other teen flicks.

Ursula Andress costarred with Elvis in *Fun in Acapulco.* The Swiss-born actress was making her first American movie though she had been appearing in Italian films since 1954.

came close to being true. To his credit, Colonel Parker for the most part kept information about Elvis's personal life out of the press.

Because of his reputation, Elvis had to be careful around his leading lady, Ursula Andress, during the making of *Fun in Acapulco.* Andress had been a Bond girl in the James Bond spy thriller *Dr. No,* but this was her first American movie. Andress was married to director/actor John Derek, who later married actress Bo Derek. Supposedly, John Derek was incredibly jealous of any man who came near his wife, so he visited the set frequently to keep an eye on her. While *Fun in Acapulco* was in production, Derek gave Andress a customized car, with "Baby, You're Indispensable" emblazoned on the steering wheel.

In *Fun in Acapulco,* Elvis plays a former trapeze artist who suffers from acrophobia after an accident causes severe injury to his partner. He settles for a job as a lifeguard in a hotel at the luxurious Mexican resort town, where he meets the hotel's social director, played by Andress. Exteriors for this musical comedy, which closely follows the established formula, were shot on location in Mexico, but Elvis never traveled South of the Border. All of his scenes were shot on the Paramount lot in Hollywood. Just before production began, a newspaper story misquoted Elvis as saying he disliked Mexico. Because of the bad publicity in the Mexican press, Hal Wallis felt it was unsafe for Elvis to shoot any scenes on location.

Fun in Acapulco became a top grosser for 1963, the year it was released. The Beatles were among the throngs of Elvis's fans who enjoyed

Though biographers and film critics continue to condemn Elvis's Hollywood career, his films have always been interesting viewing for fans, who know some of the behind-the-scenes anecdotes and tall tales.

While in Hollywood, Elvis developed a reputation for dating his costars while a movie was in production. Rumors about Elvis's relationships with actresses were repeated in fan magazines, gossip columns, and the entertainment press. Much of what was said was obviously manufactured for its publicity value, but some of the rumors were undoubtedly true or

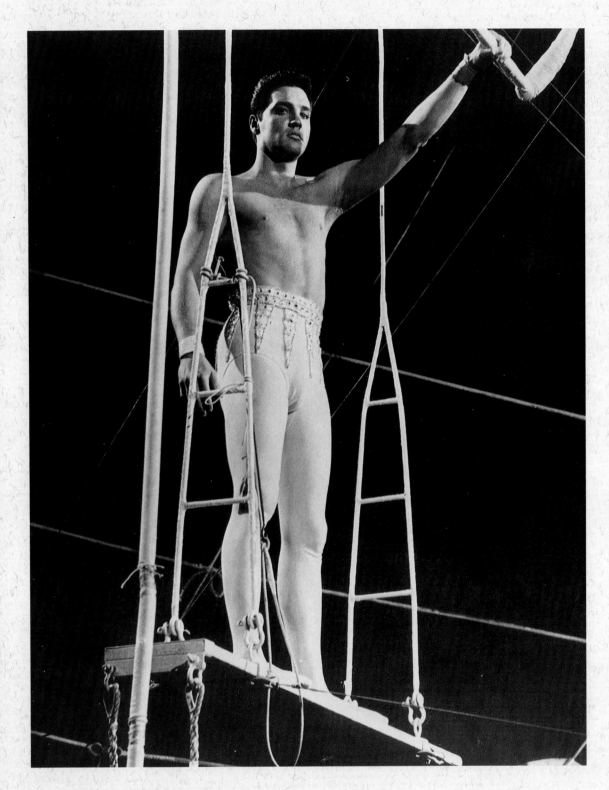

Above: The soundtrack for *Fun in Acapulco* remained on *Billboard*'s album charts for 24 weeks. **Left:** For the film, Elvis performed his own trapeze stunt, which unnerved producer Hal Wallis.

Elsa Cardenas played Elvis's other romantic interest in *Fun in Acapulco*.

Fun in Acapulco. They supposedly took time out from their first American tour to see the movie in Miami.

Elvis was not restricted to working only for Hal Wallis because the contracts they signed were not exclusive. Elvis also worked for MGM, United Artists, and Allied Artists. The producers from these other studios followed the musical comedy formula that Wallis had developed, occasionally even improving on it. *Viva Las Vegas,* produced by MGM and released in 1964, features Elvis as a race-car driver who takes a job as a waiter at the Flamingo Hotel to earn money to enter the Las Vegas Grand Prix. Ann-Margret plays a swimming instructor, who is romanced by Elvis's character and another dashing race-car driver played by Cesare Danova. The movie was shot in and around Las Vegas, using such locations as the Flamingo and Tropicana hotels, and the drag strip at Henderson, Nevada.

The inclusion of Ann-Margret made this Presley travelogue a cut above most. Ann-Margret was known at the time as "the female Elvis Presley" for her sensual, rock 'n' roll dancing style. Fans were excited about the potential screen explosion promised by the pairing of Elvis with his female namesake, and they weren't disappointed. The musical numbers in *Viva Las Vegas* are sparked by an electricity not found in other Elvis movies. The on-screen chemistry between Elvis and Ann-Margret reflected their highly publicized off-screen romance.

Of all of his relationships with his costars, Elvis's romance with Ann-Margret was probably the most serious. During the production

Ann-Margret, Elvis's love interest in *Viva, Las Vegas,* was nicknamed "the female Elvis Presley" during the early 1960s because of her sensual, high-spirited dancing style.

of *Viva Las Vegas,* Elvis and the redheaded starlet set the publicity mill grinding when they began showing up together at restaurants and clubs around Las Vegas. They shared a mutual love for motorcycles and occasionally rode together, though they were warned to be careful because an accident involving either one of them would have delayed production on the movie.

The publicity surrounding the romance was a dream come true for the producers of *Viva Las Vegas,* but it must have been difficult for Priscilla. Kept hidden from the public at Graceland, Priscilla undoubtedly saw the stories in Elvis's hometown newspaper, the *Memphis Press-Scimitar,* with headlines that

To avoid injury to either star, mattresses were placed along the paths of the motorcycles during this scene from *Viva, Las Vegas*. Elvis and Ann-Margret loved to ride motorcycles offscreen as well.

At the end of *Viva, Las Vegas*, race-car driver Lucky Jackson marries singer Rusty Martin, which was an ending the press predicted for Elvis and Ann-Margret in real life.

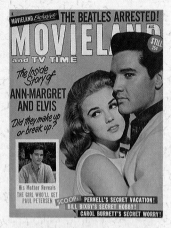

Above: The fanzines had a field day when Elvis dated Ann-Margret during the filming of *Viva, Las Vegas*. **Right:** Elvis was romantically linked with Nancy Sinatra in 1960 and during the production of *Speedway*.

blared "It Looks Like Romance for Elvis and Ann-Margret" and "Elvis Wins Love of Ann-Margret."

When *Viva Las Vegas* was first in production, Elvis was not happy to be teamed with Ann-Margret. Supposedly, someone on the production team had dated her earlier, and he was still smitten by her charm and beauty. According to members of the Memphis Mafia, this crew member assisted with photography and tended to favor Ann-Margret with more close-ups and better camera angles. When Elvis complained to the Colonel, he came to the rescue, and the crew member was soon chastised. Certain aspects of this anecdote are debatable because no crew member would have the authority to grant close-ups and change camera angles. That is the domain of the director and the cinematographer. Whatever the exact details of the story, when Elvis realized that Ann-Margret was unaware of the preferential treatment she was getting, he immediately turned on the charm and the two became fast friends. Although their romance did not work out for the long term, Elvis remained friends with Ann-Margaret for the rest of his life. Elvis married Priscilla, and Ann-Margret married actor Roger Smith, but Elvis always sent Ann-Margret flowers in the shape of a guitar on the opening night of her Las Vegas engagements.

Other costars who caught Elvis's eye included singer/dancer Juliet Prowse, who played opposite him in *G.I. Blues*. Prowse was romantically linked with Frank Sinatra at the time, whom she had met on her previous film, *Can-Can*. Fanzines circulated lurid stories claiming that Elvis had stolen Sinatra's girl,

and he would have to "pay the price." Sinatra did visit Prowse on the set of *G.I. Blues,* resulting in an embarassing situation for Elvis and his costar. Elvis was in Prowse's dressing room one day when Sinatra arrived at the studio unannounced. One of Elvis's buddy-body-guards knocked on the door to warn him that Sinatra was on the set, but, thinking it was a prank, Elvis ignored the warning. Though he laughed about it later, Elvis was surprised when Sinatra came walking through the door.

The story is of interest more for the inclusion of Frank Sinatra than it is for Juliet Prowse. Sinatra cropped up in Elvis's life an uncanny number of times. When Elvis first arrived in Hollywood, he compared his career and goals to Sinatra's in many interviews, while Sinatra was responsible for presenting the new, more mature Elvis on his television special in 1960. Both Elvis and Sinatra dated Prowse, most likely at the same time, while Elvis was romantically linked with Sinatra's daughter, Nancy, more than once. Sinatra was

Juliet Prowse, former fiancée of Frank Sinatra, dated Elvis during the production of *G.I. Blues*.

Above: Elvis dated Yvonne Craig while making *It Happened at the World's Fair*. Craig also appeared in *Kissin' Cousins*.
Below and below right: Donna Douglas and Shelley Fabares are notable for *not* dating Elvis while costarring with him.

originally offered a role in the western *Flaming Star* before the script was rewritten and Elvis became involved in the project. Finally, in the 1970s, Elvis and Sinatra recorded versions of "My Way," and both considered the song their personal anthem.

At the same time Elvis was stepping out with Juliet Prowse, he also dated Tuesday Weld, his costar in *Wild in the Country*. Weld, who was barely 17 years old when filming for *Wild in the Country* began, was already a veteran of films and television as well as of the gossip columns. For good measure, Elvis also dated wardrobe girl Nancy Sharp about this time, whom he had met while filming *Flaming Star*. Other actresses whom Elvis dated during his career in Hollywood included Joan Blackman while working on *Kid Galahad*, Yvonne Craig while shooting *It Happened at the World's Fair*, Deborah Walley during the production of *Spinout*, and Mary Ann Mobley while working on *Girl Happy*.

Some actresses are notable for not dating Elvis during film production. Donna Douglas, costar of *Frankie and Johnny*, was a religious and spiritual person who impressed Elvis because she was so well read. He admired her intellect, and he was inspired by her example to read more, particularly books on religion and philosophy. Though Elvis tried desperately to get costar Shelley Fabares to go out with him during the production of *Girl Happy*, she was heavily involved with record producer Lou Adler and later married him. In lieu of a romantic relationship, Elvis and Fabares became friends. She costarred with him in two other movies, *Spinout* and *Clambake*, and Elvis later claimed that she was his favorite costar.

Though often saddled with perky ingenues as costars, Elvis sometimes played opposite strong leading ladies and notable character actors who improved the production values of his films. A cast of big-name

stars, including Barbara Stanwyck, Leif Erickson, and Jack Albertson, made *Roustabout* one of Elvis's best vehicles. Producer Hal Wallis's solid reputation in Hollywood often helped him line up major stars for Elvis's movies. Wallis first approached Mae West for Stanwyck's role, but she declined the offer. The combination of Elvis Presley and Mae West would have made a sensational screen pairing, but West's larger-than-life persona might have detracted from the storyline, while Stanwyck's image as a tough, independent woman was well suited to the character. Edith Head, Hollywood's illustrious costume designer, did the wardrobe for the movie. She even designed a special pair of form-fitting jeans for Stanwyck.

Roustabout is set against the colorful backdrop of a small American carnival, with Elvis starring as a rakish carny hand who has a knack for finding trouble. Barbara Stanwyck discovers his singing talent and uses him to attract crowds to the midway. When filming began, tension erupted between the two major stars, but eventually they came to like and

Left: *Roustabout* starred bona fide movie star Barbara Stanwyck... **Above:** ...though Joan Freeman played Elvis's love interest.

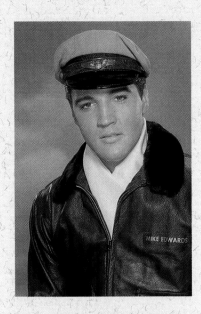

Above and below right: MGM took advantage of the publicity surrounding the Seattle World's Fair to make *It Happened at the World's Fair*. The film was written to showcase many of the fair's most popular attractions.

respect each other. Elvis said that working with Stanwyck encouraged him to become a better actor.

Elvis's musical comedies were relatively inexpensive to produce but always profitable, so Hal Wallis often used them as collateral for financing more prestigious movies. The potential profits from *Roustabout* were enough of a guarantee for investors to back Wallis's production of *Becket*, which later won an Academy Award for best adapted screenplay. After Elvis stopped making movies, he complained bitterly that this practice had made him feel used.

In 1963, the world's fair was held in Seattle, Washington. To celebrate the fair and take advantage of a well-publicized event, MGM produced *It Happened at the World's Fair*. Elvis starred with Gary Lockwood in this

musical comedy about a pair of pilots whose small plane has been attached for nonpayment of their bills. The two men end up in Seattle looking for jobs. At the world's fair, Elvis's character finds a little girl who has been separated from her family. While he searches the fairgrounds for the girl's family, the movie audience gets to see the monorail, the Space Needle, the Skyride, the Dream Car Exhibit, and many other attractions.

Vicky Tiu, who made her movie debut in *It Happened at the World's Fair*, plays the lost child. The sentimental relationship between Elvis's character and a small child became a characteristic repeated in several of his musical comedies. Like his conservative appearance and his shift to pop music, this convention helped label his movies wholesome—something the whole family could enjoy.

During the production of *It Happened at the World's Fair*, the entertainment press announced that Elvis landed the role of country singer Hank Williams in the movie biography, *Your Cheatin' Heart*. However, when the film went into production, George Hamilton was selected to portray Hank Williams. Whether the Colonel and the people at William Morris were reluctant to risk a possible flop, or whether the deal just fell through is not known, but this would not be the last time that Elvis turned down a juicy part. What a loss for music fans, who would have enjoyed watching Elvis in the life story of another musical legend.

In the early 1960s, Fort Lauderdale, Florida, became *the* vacation spot for college students during Easter break. Sensational stories began to crop up in newspaper and magazines about the dangers that lurked for coeds should they decide to try their luck in Lauderdale. Always ready to cash in on a fad, Hollywood produced several movie musicals about college kids vacationing in Florida and other resorts. A Presley travelogue, *Girl Happy,* was quickly scripted around this topical subject and released in 1965.

Girl Happy features television star Shelley Fabares as the college-age daughter of a Chicago nightclub owner. She decides to vacation in Florida over spring break, and her father hires Elvis, who plays a singer, and the members of his band to spy on his daughter while she has fun in the sun. Fabares, who played the eldest daughter on *The Donna Reed Show,* was no stranger to the pop music scene; she had recorded a number-one hit in 1962 called "Johnny Angel."

Most of the songs in *Girl Happy* are solid Elvis tunes, especially a low-down bluesy number, "Wolf Call," and an easy-sounding ballad, "You're a Puppet on a String." However, one song ranks as one of the worst tunes Elvis ever recorded. "Do the Clam" was written to accompany a dance called the Clam, which was created specially for the movie by choreographer David Winter. Winter, the dance director for the rock 'n' roll television program *Hullabaloo,* was quite familiar with modern music, but the Clam never caught on. During the mid-1960s, several dance crazes swept the nation, including the Monkey, the Pony, and the Swim. Though the Clam did not achieve the popularity of other trendy dances, it did reflect the fads and crazes of the era.

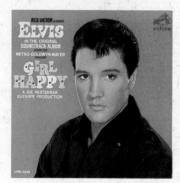

Top: Elvis played singer Rusty Wells in *Girl Happy,* which was one of the few times he portrayed a performer. **Above:** In general, the soundtrack was a solid collection of pop tunes. **Left:** However, "Do the Clam" has been cited as one of the worst songs Elvis ever recorded.

Above: *Kissin' Cousins* was long on corny musical numbers but short on production values.
Below: The soundtrack album featured three songs not included in the film. **Right:** The gimmick exploited in this film was that Elvis played two characters.

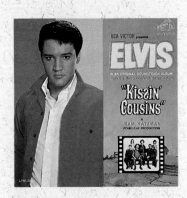

While some of Elvis's movies are not as good as others, *Kissin' Cousins,* released in 1964, is often singled out as one of Elvis's worst. This musical comedy was produced by Sam Katzman, who had a reputation for churning out low-budget movies on short schedules. Estimates on how long it took to shoot the movie vary, but everyone agrees that it took less than three weeks. The movie was budgeted at $800,000, compared to the four-million-dollar budget of *Blue Hawaii.* Little time was allotted for rehearsal, even for the musical numbers.

The farfetched storyline features Elvis in a dual role. He plays an Air Force officer who tries to persuade the Tatums, a Tennessee mountain family, to allow a missile base to be built on their land, and he also plays the backwoods son of the Tatum clan. As Officer Josh Morgan, Elvis appears with black hair; as Jody Tatum, he wears a dark blond wig, which was closer to his natural hair color. The dark-haired Elvis wins the affections of Yvonne Craig, while the blond Elvis courts Cynthia Pepper. The other characters in the movie are stereotyped Southerners. There are barefoot hillbillies, moonshiners, lazy hound dogs, man-chasing mountain girls, and pipe-smoking mammies. No wonder the movie has been criticized so often.

In addition to an offensive cast of characters, the songs for *Kissin' Cousins* sound as though they came off an assembly line. Katzman decided that since the movie had a country theme, the songs should be recorded in Nashville rather than in Hollywood, where Elvis's other soundtrack albums had been produced. But the movie's mediocre tunes are some songwriter's misguided interpretation of country-western music. The nine songs in the movie, including "Barefoot Ballad," "Pappy, Won't You Please Come Home," and "Kissin' Cousins," sound nothing like the country music that was being produced in Nashville at this time.

Kissin' Cousins was the first of Elvis's low-budget movies. After he made this movie, the shooting schedules for his musical comedies seemed to get shorter, and the budgets seemed to get smaller. Some people say that Colonel Parker felt that Elvis's popularity as a movie star was waning, so he began to seek out producers who could lower production costs. He also looked for resorts and hotels that allowed the cast and crew to stay for free. But there's no proof that the Colonel intended to lower the quality of Elvis's movies. The reverse actu-

To play country heartthrob Jody Tatum, Elvis wore a blond wig, which was closer to his natural hair color.

Sam Katzman, who had made *Kissin' Cousins* on a very low budget, also produced *Harum Scarum*. Little time or money was spent on props, costumes, or set design for either film. **Right, far right, and bottom:** Many of the costumes from *Harum Scarum* had been used in the 1944 version of *Kismet* and then retailored for the 1955 remake. Even a dagger carried by Elvis had been used in an adventure film called *Lady of the Tropics*.

ally may have been the case, and the decline in production values that went along with lower budgets and shorter schedules may have resulted in a decrease in box-office receipts.

Many talented young actors and actresses, who would go on to have prominent careers in Hollywood, were featured in secondary roles in Elvis's films. Discovering who had a small role in what Elvis movie has become a major source of enjoyment to fans. Walter Matthau, for example, was making only his sixth screen appearance when he played opposite Elvis in *King Creole* as the mobster determined to ruin everyone's lives. Barbara Eden, before popping out of a bottle in *I Dream of Jeannie*, had costarred in *Flaming Star*, while Donna Douglas played opposite Elvis in *Frankie and Johnny* before going down in the annals of pop culture as Ellie Mae Clampett in *The Beverly Hillbillies*. Ed Asner, who earned critical acclaim as television's Lou Grant and also served as president of the Screen Actors Guild, made his film debut in *Kid Galahad* as an assistant district attorney. Also appearing in *Kid Galahad* was Charles Bronson, who would later become an international star as well as one of the highest paid actors in the world. Supposedly, Elvis and Bronson did not relate well to one another during production of the film. Elvis seemed put off by Bronson's quiet demeanor, while Bronson found Elvis's constant desire to impress everyone with his expertise in karate to be annoying.

A veritable wellspring of acting talent, totally unknown at the time but who are now major stars in film and television, appeared in bits and walk-ons in Elvis's movies. Teri Garr can be spotted briefly as a background dancer

in *Viva, Las Vegas*, while Raquel Welch made her film debut in *Roustabout* as a college girl. Richard Kiel, who gained some notoriety as the steel-toothed thug known as Jaws in the James Bond films *Moonraker* and *The Spy Who Loved Me*, appeared in *Roustabout* as the carnival strong man. Comic actor Dabney Coleman had already established his humorously unsavory screen persona when he made his second film appearance in *The Trouble with Girls*.

A handful of performers who appeared in small roles in Elvis Presley movies are worth mentioning because they are offbeat or interesting in retrospect. Christina Crawford, daughter of Joan Crawford and author of the controversial biography *Mommie Dearest*, made her feature film debut in *Wild in the Country*. Crawford appeared in a bit role as a

Several TV and film stars have appeared in Elvis's movies. **Above:** Barbara Eden costarred in *Flaming Star.* **Below:** Raquel Welch (NEXT TO ELVIS) had a bit part in *Roustabout.*

local inhabitant of the small town where the action takes place. Maureen Reagan is featured in one of the most embarassing bits in any Presley picture. The daughter of former president Ronald Reagan appeared in *Kissin' Cousins* as one of the Kittyhawks, a group of man-chasing hillbilly women desperate for men. Kurt Russell, one of Hollywood's most versatile leading men, shows up in a bit role in *It Happened at the World's Fair*. Russell, who was only a child at the time, was required to kick Elvis in the shins in a comic scene that takes place on the world's fair midway. Interestingly, Russell won acclaim for his portrayal of Elvis Presley in the 1979 television biography *Elvis*, produced by Dick Clark.

Above: Maureen Reagan (FAR LEFT) appeared in a bit role in *Kissin' Cousins*. **Right:** A young Kurt Russell gives Elvis a kick in the shins in *It Happened at the World's Fair*. **Far right:** Later Russell played the singer in the 1979 TV bio *Elvis*.

Unfortunately, the music in the movies Elvis made in the 1960s was often not as good as it should have been. Elvis averaged three movies per year between 1960 and 1969, and a soundtrack album was released in conjunction with each movie. After 1964, the Colonel insisted that Elvis record only soundtrack albums. Many of the songs written for Elvis's films were done by hacks who worked for Hill and Range, the publishing house associated with RCA Records. The production values of these albums were erratic. Typically, the songs for a soundtrack album were recorded in two or three all-night sessions. Neither Colonel Parker nor anyone at RCA or Hill and Range was interested in sinking money into securing good material for Elvis when mediocre soundtrack albums were so easy to produce and sold so well. Since the system worked to everyone's advantage, there was no reason to change it. The albums and the movies promoted each other. The release of a soundtrack album reminded fans that a movie would soon be appearing in their neighborhood theater, while the movie served as a glorious advertisement for the soundtrack album.

Elvis's control of the pop, country, and rhythm-and-blues charts faded during the 1960s. After 1960, Elvis didn't have a song on the country charts until 1968, and after 1963, he would never again place a record on the R&B charts. Elvis was able to coast on his reputation until about 1965. That year, he had only one top-ten single, "Crying in the Chapel," which he actually recorded in 1960. His soundtrack albums placed in the top ten but just barely. In 1966, only one of Elvis's singles, "Love Letters," made it to the top 20. By

1967, none of Elvis's singles or albums charted anywhere near the top 20.

Though Elvis's music declined in quality, originality, and popularity during the 1960s, the decline was not as rapid as many claim, nor was *all* the music written for his films mediocre. There were some good songs recorded during that decade, even if they were for the soundtracks of his movies. Many of the tunes from *Viva Las Vegas* are comparable to those from his earlier films. Other excellent songs include the title tune from *Follow That Dream*, "Return to Sender" from *Girls, Girls, Girls*, "Rubberneckin'" from *Change of Habit*, "Wolf Call" from *Girl Happy*, "Can't Help Falling in Love" from *Blue Hawaii*, "Little

Elvis began to fade from the music charts after the Beatles changed the course of rock 'n' roll.

125

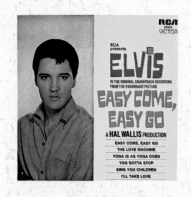

Above: The EP soundtrack for *Easy Come, Easy Go* contained all six songs from the movie.
Right: "Yoga Is as Yoga Does," one of silliest songs Elvis ever recorded, was featured in this scene from *Easy Come, Easy Go.*

Egypt" from *Roustabout,* and many more. Though there is little hard-driving rock 'n' roll or rhythm and blues in these musical numbers, Elvis's mastery of the pop-rock idiom is smooth and confident.

Unfortunately, these well-written songs tend to get lost on soundtracks that feature anywhere from six to fourteen numbers. Despite the good songs, there is no escaping the fact that Elvis recorded some clunkers during the 1960s. Among the most ridiculous are "No Room to Rhumba in a Sports Car" from *Fun in Acapulco,* "Fort Lauderdale Chamber of Commerce" from *Girl Happy,* "Queenie Wahini's Papaya" from *Paradise, Hawaiian Style,* "Yoga Is as Yoga Does" from *Easy Come, Easy Go,* "Barefoot Ballad" from *Kissin Cousins,* "He's Your Uncle, Not Your Dad" from *Speedway,* and "Petunia, the Gardener's Daughter" from *Frankie and Johnny.*

RCA did not market or package Elvis's albums very wisely. His soundtrack albums were a hodge-podge of songs that lacked unity and consistency, and the Colonel and the people at RCA were determined to saturate the market by releasing material at an extremely rapid rate. It was not unusual for RCA to release a Presley soundtrack while an earlier one was still on the charts, though standard practice was for a performer to get as much mileage from an album as possible before releasing the next.

If Elvis grew dissatisfied with Hollywood, then why did he continue to star in these movies and to record the music featured in them? The most logical explanation involves their financial success. Most of Elvis's albums and films secured a profit no matter how hastily they were manufactured, which served to validate the path he and the Colonel chose for his career. Also, the Colonel continually tied him up with three-film contracts with a number of studios, so even when Elvis decided to stop making movies around 1968, he was contractually obligated to star in several more.

Despite the decline in box-office revenue for Elvis's films at the end of the 1960s, everyone benefited financially from these vehicles. The budgets of Elvis's films were planned so that 50 percent of the total budget was allotted for his salary, and he received a percentage of the profits. Parker received 25 percent of Presley's gross income and whatever he could negotiate as technical adviser, while Abe Lastfogel of William Morris received ten percent off the top of any film deal.

Colonel Parker understood the key to the financial success of the films when he told a scriptwriter that there were a quarter of a million die-hard Elvis Presley fans willing to see each movie three times. The fans believed that Elvis's charisma transcended any mediocre material he was given. When the lines formed outside the box offices, the people in those lines came to see Elvis and nothing else.

The many biographers and detractors who search for an explanation as to why Elvis continued to star in the Presley travelogues need look no further than this 1966 fan letter:

"Dear Elvis, You're movie played two weeks at Loew's, and I saw it at least twice a day. I can't hardly wait to see it again when it comes to the neighborhood. I have seen it 29 times."

Above: This fanzine refers to Elvis's nickname, "the Million Dollar Actor." In the mid-1960s, he was the highest-paid screen actor. **Below left:** Elvis shows the *Girls, Girls, Girls* script to his pet chimp, Scatter. Elvis became so disillusioned with his later films that he stopped reading scripts. **Below:** Colonel Tom Parker and Priscilla join Elvis on the set of *Stay Away, Joe*. Parker was named technical adviser on 24 of Elvis's films.

CHAPTER SEVEN

COMEBACK

"IN 1968...ELVIS MAKES THE NBC-SINGER SPECIAL, A COMBINATION OF SLICK SKITS AND ROUGH, INTIMATE CONCERT FOOTAGE PRODUCED BY STEVE BINDER. IT WAS A SMASH. THE ADJECTIVES USED TO DESCRIBE HIM—DEVASTING, KILLER, ANIMAL—MAKE YOU WONDER WHAT WOMEN WANT."

—*Jill Pearlman, ELVIS FOR BEGINNERS*

Producer Hal Wallis ended his association with Elvis and Colonel Tom Parker in 1966 after the production of *Easy Come, Easy Go.* Elvis continued to make movies for other studios as he had been doing all along. Some of these movies are mediocre at best, including the lackluster *Double Trouble* and *Clambake* from 1967, and the ridiculously far-fetched *Live a Little, Love a Little,* released in 1968.

That year, Elvis decided to stop making movies as soon as he had fulfilled his existing contracts. Curiously, his last three movies, all released in 1969, broke away from the formula of the Presley travelogues. Why Elvis made this change so late in his movie career is not really known. Perhaps he still had the desire to mature as an actor and wanted one last attempt at serious roles before he left Hollywood, or maybe the Colonel thought a different type of storyline might score big at the box office at this time. Most likely, the deals were simply too good for the Colonel to pass up. Whatever the reason, *Charro, The Trouble with Girls,* and *Change of Habit* represent a significant difference from Elvis's other movies.

Charro, in particular, was a radical departure because the film is a low-budget western with Elvis in the title role as a former outlaw. The story follows Charro, who's now on the side of law and order, as he stands up to the members of his old gang. They try to frame him for the theft of a valuable cannon that belongs to the Mexican government. Elvis's role is not glamorous. Throughout the movie, he looks unkempt and wears the same dusty outfit. Elvis is barely recognizable behind a scruffy beard, and he sings no songs other than the title tune, which is heard as the opening credits roll by. The poster used to advertise the movie exploits this new turn in Elvis's movie career by touting *Charro* as "a different kind of role…a different kind of man."

The background score for *Charro* was not written by anyone connected with Elvis, RCA, or Hill and Range. Instead, the movie's music was scored and conducted by Hugo Montenegro, who received critical acclaim for his memorable theme for Clint Eastwood's Italian western *The Good, the Bad, and the Ugly.* The director of *Charro,* Charles Marquis, who also produced and scripted the movie, was obviously trying to capture the tense atmosphere and gritty look of the Italian westerns that

Below and opposite page: The western *Charro* represented a departure from the typical Presley picture. Unfortunately, it came too late in Elvis's film career to make a difference.

Above: Anissa Jones, Pepe Brown, Marlyn Mason, and Elvis take a bow in *The Trouble with Girls.* Anissa (FAR LEFT) later starred as Buffy on the TV sitcom *A Family Affair.* **Opposite page:** *The Trouble with Girls* was mired by several meandering subplots, including one involving Sheree North and Edward Andrews.

were so popular in the 1960s. Elvis's character emulated Clint Eastwood's Man with No Name with his beard and rugged appearance, and Hugo Montenegro's score made the movie sound like an Italian western. Unfortunately, Marquis, who had directed and produced television westerns, lacked the vision to to carry it off. The film is slow moving and dull, and it was not well received by fans and critics.

At first glance, *The Trouble with Girls* may seem a throwback to the Presley travelogue, but a closer look reveals an offbeat film that is not typical of Elvis. The story takes place in the 1920s and is about a traveling chautauqua, which is a rolling canvas college that featured assorted classes in culture, reading, music, and other subjects. Chautauquas traveled from town to town, bringing culture to rural areas and isolated villages. The name derives from

Chautauqua, New York, where a 12-day study program for Sunday school teachers had been set up in 1873.

Although Elvis, as the manager of the chautauqua, is at the center of the movie, the storyline is taken up by the secondary characters. A couple of poor kids desperately want to be in the talent competition sponsored by the chautauqua; there is an illicit love affair that ends in murder; and there are other misadventures that have little to do with Elvis's character. Elvis's role in the movie is to romance the character played by Marlyn Mason. Elvis doesn't make an appearance in the film until about a third of the way through, when he strolls into a scene wearing a gleaming white suit and dapper white hat. More handsome than ever, he sports a long hairstyle with sideburns, which was more like the fashion of the 1960s than the 1920s. Despite his attractive appearance, Elvis's character is little more than an elaborate plot device that functions to tie the various stories together.

Elvis's last narrative feature was the melodrama *Change of Habit,* which costarred television favorite Mary Tyler Moore. Elvis plays a devoted doctor who works in a clinic in a big-city slum. Three young nuns, including Moore, are assigned to the ghetto to do social work. They decide to exchange their old-fashioned habits for modern dress, and Elvis falls in love with Moore, not realizing that she's a nun. In the final scene, Moore must choose between Elvis and the Church. A true cliffhanger, the film concludes without revealing which path she takes, letting the audience decide for themselves.

As Dr. John Carpenter in *Change of Habit,* Elvis played a dedicated professional rather than one of the footloose free spirits he had portrayed so often in the past.

Elvis's character, a dedicated professional, was quite different from the free-spirited girl chasers he was accustomed to playing. *Change of Habit* featured only a handful of songs, including the popular hit "Rubberneckin'." Elvis seemed comfortable in the role, despite the change in character type, and reviewers commented on his relaxed and fluid performance. Even though *Change of Habit* showed a profit at the box office, it made a much bigger splash on television when it was shown on NBC's *Friday Night at the Movies* in 1972.

Elvis blamed the decrease in record sales and his loss of popularity, particularly among the younger generation, on his films. One mediocre vehicle after another had strained the devotion of Elvis's long-time supporters and failed to bring him many new fans. Saddled with film and recording contracts, which were endlessly negotiated and manipulated by the Colonel so that no matter how poor the product, there was still a substantial profit, Elvis no longer felt challenged by the entertainment industry by the end of the 1960s.

At this time, Elvis desired a change not only in his career but also in his private life. Priscilla had been living at Graceland for several years, maintaining a low profile to keep the press away, but on May 1, 1967, Elvis brought his princess bride out of hiding. He and Priscilla were married at the Aladdin Hotel in Las Vegas. It wasn't a fairy-tale wedding, but they were both very happy to be married. The double-ring ceremony lasted only eight minutes and took place in the suite of one of the Colonel's friends. Only a few of

Above: Elvis obliges the fans by signing autographs during a break in the shooting of his last film, *Change of Habit.* **Left:** While Elvis was making films during the 1960s, Priscilla Beaulieu remained at Graceland out of the public eye. Here, Elvis and Priscilla pose with Minnie Mae Presley, Elvis's grandmother.

Above, above right, and right:
Elvis Aron Presley and Priscilla
Ann Beaulieu were wed in a private ceremony on May 1, 1967,
at the Aladdin Hotel in Las Vegas.

Left and below left: Immediately following the ceremony, a reception was held in one of the hotel ballrooms, mostly for the benefit of the press. **Below:** The newlyweds catch a private plane to Palm Springs, where they honeymooned.

137

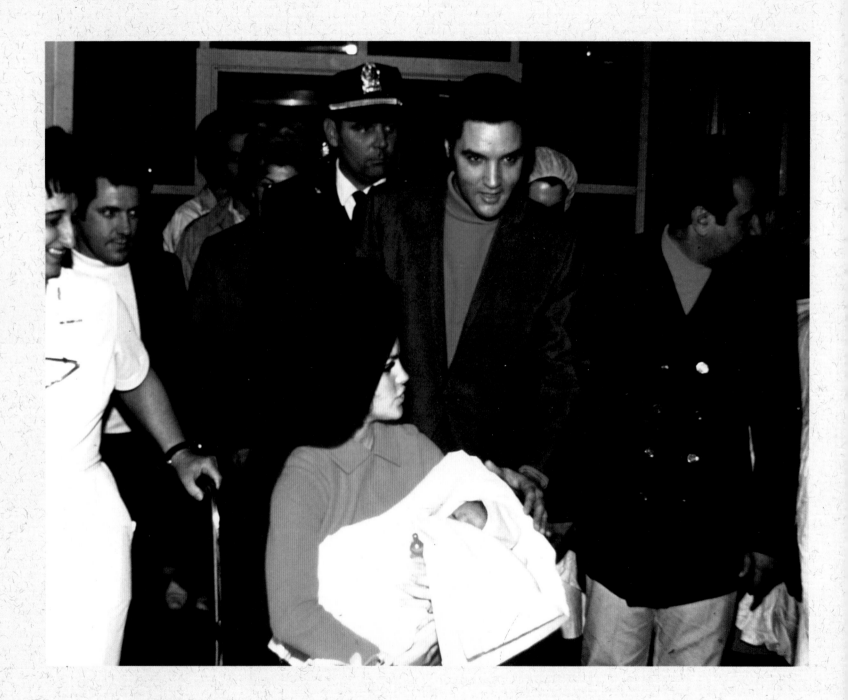

Opposite page: Fans still marvel at the fact that Elvis and Priscilla's only child, Lisa Marie, was born nine months to the day after they were married. **Above left and left:** Elvis was a loving father as indicated by these candid snapshots. **Above:** This was one of the professional photos released to the press after Lisa Marie's birth.

Above: Elvis's *'68 Comeback Special* was sponsored by Singer and originally titled *Singer Presents Elvis.* **Below:** Plans for the special are announced at a press conference by Bones Howe (musical producer), Steve Binder (producer and director), Elvis, and Bob Finkel (executive producer).

Elvis's buddies were allowed to witness the actual event, causing some dissension in the ranks of the Memphis Mafia. Joe Esposito and Marty Lacker served as best men, and Priscilla's sister, Michelle, was the maid of honor. After the ceremony, there was a breakfast reception for 100 at the Aladdin, which was an event held primarily for the press. Elvis and Priscilla honeymooned in Palm Springs, California, and then split their time between Graceland and their new home in Beverly Hills. On February 1, 1968, nine months to the day after Elvis and Priscilla were married, Lisa Marie Presley was born.

Shortly after he was married, Elvis reported to the set at MGM to begin filming on *Speedway.* Although many of Elvis's biographies have suggested that Elvis was not comfortable with his marriage, actor Bill Bixby (Elvis's costar) recalls that Elvis was content and happy, even ecstatic at times. He was thinner than he had been in his last few pictures and seemed to have settled down. The years of Elvis's marriage (1968 to 1972) are also the years of his last extended period of creativity.

In 1968, Colonel Parker announced plans for an Elvis Presley television special on NBC. The show was planned for Christmastime, and it would be Elvis's first television appearance in eight years. Parker's plans for the special were typical of his approach to show business—get as much as you can for as little money and effort as possible. The Colonel wanted Elvis to walk onto a set decorated for Christmas, introduce himself, and then humbly sing as many well-known Christmas carols as he could fit into an hour. For a finale, Elvis was supposed to wish everyone a happy holiday and then walk off the set. With that many Christmas carols involved, the Colonel was probably planning to make one or two albums from the special as a bonus to the arrangement.

Fortunately for Elvis and his fans, the Colonel did not get his way. NBC hired Steve Binder, a pioneer in translating the dynamism of rock 'n' roll to television, to produce and direct Elvis's prime-time special. Binder's credits include creating and directing *The T.A.M.I. Show,* a 1964 concert movie featuring the Supremes, Chuck Berry, James Brown, the Rolling Stones, Gerry and the Pacemakers, and Smokey Robinson and the Miracles.

Binder also directed the weekly rock 'n' roll variety series *Hullabaloo*. When he heard about the Colonel's idea for Elvis to make a conventional Christmas special, Binder flatly refused to go along with it. This placed him permanently on the Colonel's list of enemies.

A fan of both Elvis and modern music, Binder felt it was time for the King of Rock 'n' Roll to return from exile and snatch his crown from those who had surreptitiously slipped away with it. Binder wanted Elvis to make a statement with this special. He wanted the show to say something about Elvis's musical roots and about the musical style he had helped develop in the 1950s.

If Binder was to succeed in turning his ideas for the special into reality, he had to secure Elvis's cooperation and trust, even if that meant encouraging Elvis to go against the Colonel. Binder pushed Elvis to challenge himself again for the first time since the early 1960s. As a way to impress upon Elvis that his currency had deflated among younger audiences, Binder challenged Elvis to walk down Sunset Strip to see if there would be any reaction from the young people who hung out there. Elvis had kept himself totally isolated from the public since he was discharged from the army, and he was reluctant to expose himself to an uncontrolled crowd. But Binder prevailed, and he, Elvis, and several members of the Memphis Mafia strolled nonchalantly down the Strip. No one noticed. Elvis tried subtly to attract attention to himself, but still no one indicated that they knew who he was. If anyone on Sunset Strip recognized Elvis, they didn't seem to care. Even though the

A publicity shot for *The '68 Comeback Special* shows a fit and handsome Elvis on the verge of a career change.

Elvis sings in one of the special's many production numbers, which very loosely tell the story of a young guitar player who finds fame and fortune.

crowd on the strip was hardly a group of typical Americans, this experience helped convince Elvis that he needed a unique vehicle to put him on top again. In the battle of wills that ensued between Parker and Binder, Elvis sided with Binder.

Going against the Colonel's advice and wishes wasn't easy for Elvis, and Parker didn't take it well. The Colonel was at Binder's throat throughout the production. He insisted on mispronouncing the young director's name as "Bindle" as a way of illustrating his contempt. The conflict came to a head in a disagreement over the show's finale. Parker was determined to close the special with "Silent Night," while Binder wanted to end with an original song. Binder defied the Colonel one more time and asked the show's choral director, Earl Brown, to write something special for the finale. Brown came up with a powerful song called "If I Can Dream," which featured a spiritual message in a hip, soulful arrangement. After Brown played the song for Elvis several times, Elvis agreed it would make a dramatic finale.

Even though Elvis trusted Binder's concept for the show, he never openly defied the Colonel. He would merely listen to Parker's demands and nod his head in agreement from time to time. But when Parker was out of the room, Elvis cooperated fully with Binder. Elvis kept assuring the young director that everything was going to be all right. To get around the Colonel, Binder supposedly shot Elvis singing "Silent Night" though he had no intention of including the song in the special. Parker had successfully guided Elvis's career for 13 years by this time, making him a multi-

millionaire and a household name in the process. It must have been incredibly difficult for Elvis to question the Colonel's judgement and ultimately side against him.

Binder's first concept for the show included a storyline about an innocent young musician who goes out into the world to seek his fortune only to find that the world is a wicked and sordid place. Elvis was to be the young man, and the story was going to be told entirely through song and dance. Binder wanted the opening segment to take place in a brothel, but the NBC censors wouldn't allow it, so Binder decided to scrap the concept and come up with something else.

In its final form, the special is a series of polished production numbers designed to illustrate the essence of Elvis's music. These musical numbers alternate with segments that were filmed before a live studio audience made up mostly of women. For these live seg-

The high point of the special was the live segments in which Elvis sang before a studio audience accompanied by Scotty Moore and D.J. Fontana, among others.

The '68 Comeback Special was aired December 3, 1968, and was the highest-rated program of that week. Bob Finkel won a Peabody Award for his work on the show.

The black leather outfit worn by Elvis during the live segments was the work of Bill Belew, who later designed several of Elvis's jumpsuits.

The Claude Thompson Dancers backed Elvis in the special's production numbers, but there were no other performers on the program.

ments, Elvis wore a black leather jacket and pants with his jet black hair slightly slicked back—an effect that recalled an earlier persona but did not duplicate it. Elvis had always been an attractive man, but on this program he was radiantly handsome and his voice had never been better. He was joined by two of his original backup musicians, D.J. Fontana and Scotty Moore. Binder wanted Elvis to sing some of his old hits and reminisce about his early career. He was supposed to talk to the audience informally, giving his opinions on modern music and telling stories about the good old days, but Elvis couldn't quite bring himself to be so open. Instead, he joked casually with Moore and Fontana and let his music speak for him. Elvis sang many of his old songs, including "Jailhouse Rock," "Love Me Tender," and "Lawdy, Miss Clawdy," but he sang with such vigor and freshness that the songs sounded different, almost new. Elvis's vocal range had lowered through the years, and he had gained confidence and control. In part, this explains why the songs sounded new. Yet, on another level, Elvis was singing with an intensity of purpose—to restore his place as the King of Rock 'n' Roll.

Although recorded during the summer, the special didn't air until December 3, 1968. Originally titled *Singer Presents Elvis,* the special is now simply referred to as *The '68 Comeback Special.* It was the highest-rated program for that week, and critics praised Elvis's performance, remarking on his magic and charisma as an entertainer. The accompanying album was received just as favorably. More importantly, *The '68 Comeback Special*

represents a true turning point in Elvis's career. He had been resting on his laurels as a pop-singing movie idol, but he had long ceased to light any sparks or stir any passions. Elvis needed a challenge to push him in a new direction, and Binder issued that challenge. Elvis met it with an intensity he would rarely match again. *The '68 Comeback Special* was literally his finest hour.

For the finale, Elvis sang "If I Can Dream," which was written especially for him by W. Earl Brown. As a single, "If I Can Dream" became a million-seller and reached number 12 on the charts.

CHAPTER EIGHT

LIVE ONSTAGE

"ELVIS REMAINS ONE OF THE QUINTESSENTIAL AMERICAN POP STARS, GAUDY, GARISH, COMPROMISED IN HIS MIDDLE AGE IN COMMERCIAL CONSIDERATION, YET GIFTED WITH AN ENORMOUS TALENT AND A CHARISMATIC APPEAL BEYOND MERE NOSTALGIA. PRESLEY REMAINS A TRUE AMERICAN ARTIST— ONE OF THE GREATEST IN AMERICAN POPULAR MUSIC, A SINGER OF NATIVE BRILLIANCE AND A PERFORMER OF MAGNETIC DIMENSIONS."

—*Jim Millar*, ROLLING STONE

Above and below right: Excited by the challenge and success of *The '68 Comeback Special*, Elvis was eager to pump some life into his recording career.

The challenge of *The '68 Comeback Special* and its subsequent success inspired Elvis to record new material that sounded more contemporary than what was offered on the movie soundtracks.

Elvis had begun to move away from the style of his soundtrack recordings in the fall of 1967. Under the direction of RCA record producer Felton Jarvis, he recorded the country rock sounds of "Big Boss Man," released in 1967, and "Guitar Man," released in January of 1968. These two singles are considered the forerunners of the songs that brought Elvis success on the charts in the late 1960s and early 1970s. "Guitar Man" and "Big Boss Man" were both successful enough to be featured in production numbers on the comeback special. During this 1967 session at RCA, Elvis also recorded "Hi-Heel Sneakers," "You Don't Know Me," "Too Much Monkey Business," and "U.S. Male."

RCA released a single of "If I Can Dream" in conjunction with the comeback special, and Elvis proved once again that his recordings could move up the charts. By January of 1969, it had reached number 12 on the pop listings, making it Elvis's biggest single since 1965. The soundtrack album from the special, titled simply *Elvis*, reached number eight on the album charts for pop music.

Eager to record more new material, Elvis booked ten days at American Sound Studios, a small independent studio in Memphis. Elvis's decision to use a small studio over RCA's Nashville facilities was not unusual. At that time, many independent studios offered recording stars a relaxed atmosphere and conscientious attention to detail that were not always available at larger recording facilities. By 1969, American Sound Studios had gained a reputation as one of the most successful independent studios in the industry. Chips Moman, one of the owners who also served as an engineer, was Elvis's producer. He had experience working with chart-topping singers from many fields of music. In addition to Moman's expertise, the studio had a great house band that was made up of musicians who were well-versed in country-western music, rhythm and blues, and rock 'n' roll. Elvis felt at home in American Sound Studios because the place had a rough, down-home atmosphere not unlike Sun Studios in the 1950s.

Moman helped Elvis develop the style and sound he would use for the rest of his career. The musicians who played in the house band at the studio had been influenced by Elvis

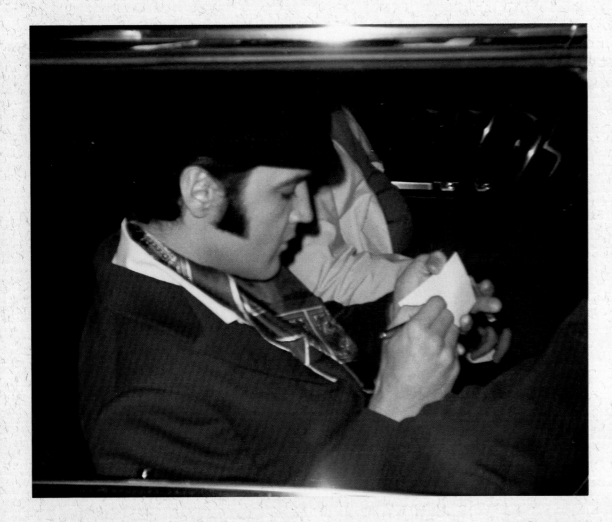

In 1956, Elvis's sideburns had caused quite a stir in the North, where they were considered unusual and even vulgar. But, during the late 1960s, he looked very much in fashion.

during the 1950s and could be considered his musical heirs. They shared his Southern roots and seemed to understand fully the direction his music was taking. The style Elvis worked out with Chips Moman and the band was not straightforward rock 'n' roll, but it wasn't traditional country-western music or rhythm and blues either. Elvis's style took something from all these kinds of music, yet his work transcended specific musical categories to form a sound wholly unique. No song shows this more clearly than the all-encompassing sound of "Suspicious Minds" and its seemingly endless crescendo. Elvis's delivery of this song represents the essence of his later musical style that developed after 1969.

Elvis planned to record for ten days during January 1969, but he had laryngitis and was able to work for only six days. Elvis still managed to record 36 tracks. The session was so successful that Elvis returned to American Sound Studios for five more days of recording the following month. During these two recording sessions at American Sound

Studios, Elvis did some of the best work of his career. He recorded three top-ten singles—"Suspicious Minds," "Don't Cry Daddy," and "In the Ghetto"—as well as "Kentucky Rain," "Only the Strong Survive," and "I'm Movin' On." The recordings made during these sessions were released on two albums: *From Elvis in Memphis* and *From Memphis to Vegas/From Vegas to Memphis.*

The 36 tracks recorded at American Sound Studios cover a wide range of musical styles from country tunes to contemporary soul music. The best songs didn't come from Hill and Range, the music publisher associated with RCA; they were written by young, independent songwriters, including Mark James, Mac Davis, and the team of Eddie Rabbitt and Dick Heard. It's unlikely that Colonel Parker and his associates, including Freddy Bienstock of Hill and Range, were very pleased by Elvis's decision to record material

they didn't control. When Elvis recorded songs that had been written by songwriters who were not under contract to Hill and Range or songs that had not been acquired by Elvis Presley Music, Elvis and his management team did not receive publishing royalties. The Colonel and Bienstock are said to have been particularly upset about Elvis's determination to record "Suspicious Minds," because Chips Moman owned the publishing rights to it. Supposedly, Parker tried to pressure Moman into giving him a piece of the rights, but Moman refused. Parker even threatened to persuade RCA not to release the song if Elvis and Moman went ahead and recorded it against the Colonel's wishes. But the matter was quickly settled when an RCA executive arrived in Memphis and realized that the song had the potential to become a hit.

The year 1969 became a seminal year for Elvis Presley in the way that 1956 and 1960 had been. Just as the events in those years had determined a certain image for Elvis, so did the events of 1969 point Elvis toward a new image and a new sound. His dynamic recordings from the first half of that year helped steer him toward that goal, but it was his smash engagement that summer in Las Vegas that constructed the image that would stay with him for the rest of his career.

After Elvis felt the excitement of singing for a live audience during the performance segment of the comeback special, he was excited to return to the stage. In the early summer of 1969, Elvis was invited to play the new International Hotel in Las Vegas. The main room of the hotel had not yet been opened, and Elvis was asked to do the honors.

The International Hotel asked Elvis to open its new main room in the summer of 1969. Elvis declined to open the room, but he was the *second* performer to appear there.

When the Colonel decided that Elvis shouldn't take the chance of making his live comeback on an untested stage, Barbra Streisand was booked to open the main room of the International in July, while Elvis was scheduled for August. Although reports on the exact amount of his salary vary widely, Elvis was paid a half million dollars for four weeks. The marquis read simply "ELVIS."

Elvis had not appeared before a live audience since 1961, when his music had been much simpler. For his return to live performing, Elvis chose not to re-create his earlier image or sound. Instead, he planned his act on a broad scale. Elvis's first band back in 1956 had consisted of a guitarist, a bass player, and a drummer. For his Las Vegas performances, he was joined on stage by the Imperials (a pop/gospel quartet), the Sweet Inspirations (a female backup trio), a rock band, and a 35-piece orchestra. The members of his rock band included the well-known Southern blues guitarist James Burton, drummer Ronnie Tutt, bassist Jerry Scheff, keyboard player Larry Muhoberack, and guitarists/vocalists John Wilkinson and Charlie Hodge. (Hodge had been part of the Memphis Mafia since the days when he and Elvis were in the army together.) Part of the reason for such an extensive entourage was undoubtedly due to the large room Elvis was to perform in at the International, but the enormous sound created by Elvis and his musical entourage seemed aurally symbolic of Colonel Parker's favorite billing for his boy—"the World's Greatest Entertainer."

Elvis was frightfully nervous about staging his comeback to live performances in Las Vegas, because he had bombed there when he

Left and below: Elvis jokes with the media at a press conference to promote his engagement at the International.

show-business event of the year. Kirk Kerkorian, owner of the International at that time, planned to send his own plane to New York to fly in the rock press for opening night. The list of celebrities who planned to attend Elvis's opening included Pat Boone, Fats Domino, Wayne Newton, Dick Clark, Ann-Margret, George Hamilton, Angie Dickinson, and Henry Mancini. Elvis personally invited Sam Phillips, the man who had helped him develop his raw talent into a unique musical style.

On July 31, 1969, Elvis performed in front of a sold-out crowd at the International. To the hard-pounding strains of "Baby, I Don't Care," Elvis walked on stage. There was no emcee to introduce him. He grabbed the microphone, struck a familiar pose from the past, and snapped his leg back and forth. The crowd jumped from their chairs to give him a standing ovation before he sang one note. The audience of 2,000 began to whistle, applaud

Above right: The Colonel outdid himself promoting Elvis's International appearance. He strolled around the lobby of the hotel in a topcoat that was covered with Elvis's name. **Far right:** Elvis strikes a pose during one of his performances at the International in August 1969.

appeared at the New Frontier Hotel in April 1956. The sting of his failure had not diminished with the passing years. Though he did have time for several rehearsals before his engagement at the International, there was no opportunity to iron out any kinks before a live audience, adding to his anxiety. Elvis may have been frightened, but Colonel Parker was in his element as he began promoting his boy all over Las Vegas. He rented every available billboard and took out full-page ads in the local and trade papers. The lobby of the International was filled with Elvis Presley souvenirs—T-shirts, straw boaters, records, and even stuffed animals. The Colonel made sure that Elvis's return to the stage would be the

furiously, and pound on the tables. Some people stood on their chairs. When the ovation began to subside, Elvis launched into "Blue Suede Shoes" with such fury that ten years of his movie music melted away.

Elvis looked unbelievably handsome that night. He was dressed in a modified karate suit made specially for him out of black mohair. He was thinner than he had been in his last few films, and his blue-black hair reached down past his collar. Elvis's sideburns were the longest they had been since the 1950s. Never one to take himself too seriously, Elvis joked with the crowd about the old days and the old songs. At one point, he decided to dedicate his next number to the audience and the staff at the International: "This is the only song I could think of that really expresses my feeling toward the audience," he said in all earnestness, before bursting into "Hound Dog." Elvis closed his act with "What'd I Say" from *Viva, Las Vegas,* and again the sold-out crowd gave him a standing ovation. Elvis came back for an encore and sang "Can't Help Falling in Love," the song he closed every show with for the rest of his career.

Backstage after the performance, many celebrities and well-wishers, including Cary Grant, were on hand to congratulate Elvis on his triumphant return to live performance. Priscilla Beaulieu Presley, in her account of her life with Elvis, reveals a touching story about Colonel Parker. At this moment of great personal and professional triumph for his one and only client, the Colonel pushed his way backstage. Everyone could see that tears were welling up in his eyes. Where was "his boy" he wanted to know. As Elvis emerged from his dressing room, the two men embraced, too overcome with emotion to say anything. There have been many stories about Colonel Tom Parker over the years, many of them illustrating his greed, his mistakes, or his ruthlessness. Yet no story reveals the complexity of the relationship between Elvis and the Colonel like this one.

Most members of the rock 'n' roll press, many of whom were teenagers when Elvis began his career, were ecstatic about his return to the stage and expressed their enthusiasm in glowing reviews. *Rolling Stone* magazine declared Elvis to be supernatural while *Variety* proclaimed him a superstar. *Newsweek* praised him for his staying power, remarking, "It was hard to believe he was 34 and no longer 19 years old...."

Vernon Presley joined his son in Las Vegas for the four-week engagement at the International.

Above and below: Elvis met Tom Jones in Las Vegas in 1968, and the two singers became lifelong friends. They attended each other's stage shows and emulated each other's performance mannerisms.

The day after Elvis's opening night, the Colonel sat down with the general manager of the International to discuss the enormous success of the performance. The hotel offered Elvis a five-year contract to play two months a year—February and August—at a salary of one million dollars per year. In his typical flamboyant style, the Colonel took out a pen and began scribbling specific terms on the red tablecloth. When he finished, he asked the general manager to sign the cloth to close the deal. Although the "red tablecloth deal" has become a show business legend, Parker has been criticized for locking Elvis into a long-term contract that didn't take inflation into account.

Six months after his first Las Vegas show, Elvis returned to the International for another month of sold-out performances. During this engagement, Elvis wore a jumpsuit on stage.

Bill Belew, who had designed the black leather outfit for the comeback special, designed a white jumpsuit for this occasion. The costume was slashed down the front to reveal the chest, fitted closely at the waist, and belled out at the legs, which was the fashion of the day. The costume's high collar was inset with semi-precious jewels, and Elvis wore gold and diamond rings on the fingers of both hands. A macramé karate belt made of gold- and pearl-colored strands accentuated his slender waist.

Dean Martin attended the opening night of Elvis's second Las Vegas engagement. Elvis sang "Everybody Loves Somebody Sometime" as a tribute to Martin, the pop singer he had always admired. Elvis altered his repertoire for this engagement by emphasizing his current recordings and including some contemporary country and rock ballads. He limited the older material to a few key places during the show, or he covered it in a medley-style arrangement. He was determined not to rest on his laurels so he focused his act on his new material and his new sound, which he had developed with the help of Chips Moman at American Sound Studios.

Elvis was not merely a nostalgia act, although the success of his comeback was probably enhanced by the revival of 1950s music that began in the late 1960s. Many performers who had helped develop the rock 'n' roll sound and attitude reaped the benefits of this renewed interest in the roots of rock music. Bill Haley and the Comets, Chuck Berry, and Jerry Lee Lewis were touring once again and attracting large crowds. Elvis's success at this time not only benefitted from the rock-nostalgia craze but undoubtedly influenced it. Yet, Elvis was careful to keep his material new and varied. He didn't identify himself with the rock 'n' roll revival, and his show was never considered to be merely an oldies act.

Following his success in Las Vegas, Elvis took his act on tour. For Elvis's first show on the road, Colonel Parker arranged for him to appear in the Houston Astrodome in conjunction with the Texas Livestock Show. The logic behind choosing such a large arena was simple: Elvis as "the World's Greatest Entertainer" should appear only in magnificent coliseums or showplaces. Besides, Texas had always been good to Elvis. In 1955, East Texas had been the scene of a great surge of Elvis-mania, which helped boost his early career. To return this kindness and perhaps to ensure a sellout, tickets for Elvis's engagement at the Astrodome were greatly reduced in price, with some seats selling for as little as one dollar.

Despite the boost in confidence from his Vegas victories, Elvis was overwhelmed by the size of the Astrodome and the thought of having to please 44,500 people. Referring to the Astrodome as an "ocean," he worried about losing some of his energy and dynamism in such a vast arena. Again his fears proved unfounded because the Astrodome sold out each night of his engagement, and the local music critics raved about his personal charisma and his exciting act. For the first time since the 1950s, Elvis was mobbed after his show in a frightening example of mob hysteria. His limousine had been parked by the stage door so Elvis could make a rapid get-

Elvis socialized with a number of fellow entertainers while performing in Las Vegas, including Glen Campbell. Campbell had played guitar and sang backup on the soundtrack of *Viva, Las Vegas*.

Above: While on tour, Elvis always had a car waiting behind the arena or stage area so that he could make a quick exit. **Right:** At Priscilla's suggestion, Elvis began to wear jumpsuits on stage because they were comfortable.

away, but the fans were able to reach the car quickly. They surrounded the vehicle; some tried to shove flowers and gifts into the doors and windows while others just wanted to touch their idol.

After the success in Houston, Elvis continued to tour. He was usually on the road for several weeks out of a month, in addition to playing Las Vegas in February and August. His touring schedule was grueling. By 1971, Elvis was on the road more than most other acts in show business. He would tour for three weeks at a time, taking no days off and doing two shows on Saturday and Sunday. He would rest

for a few weeks and then repeat the cycle. Elvis usually played one night stands, meaning every performance was scheduled for a different arena. Often Elvis and his entourage would arrive in a city and depart again in less than 24 hours. Such a demanding schedule took its toll in terms of Elvis's desire to update or change the material in his act. Eventually, his performances became standardized, even routine. Despite this, Elvis's concerts were almost always sold out.

Elvis's return to concert performing probably contributed to the disintegration of his marriage to Priscilla. Gone from Graceland much of the time while touring in concert, Elvis saw less of Priscilla and his daughter, Lisa Marie, as his career and lifestyle took a different direction. The horrendous pace of performing in a different city every night made traveling together difficult, and Elvis enforced a no-wives rule while on the road, which applied to himself and all members of the Memphis Mafia. Priscilla left Elvis in early 1972, and Elvis sued for divorce the following August. Elvis's lawyer succinctly summed up the problem when he released this statement: "Elvis has been spending six months a year on the road, which put a tremendous strain on the marriage." In October 1973, the couple were officially divorced, but it was an amicable split. They held hands during the divorce proceedings and walked out of the courtroom arm in arm.

A typical Presley concert of the 1970s was more like a series of rituals and cermonies than a performance by a mere entertainer. Making his entrance to Richard Strauss's *Also*

Above: Elvis's frequent touring took its toll on his family life. **Top left:** Priscilla and Elvis walk out of the courtroom after their divorce is finalized. **Bottom left:** After the divorce, Priscilla pursued various careers, including fashion design and acting.

sprach Zarathustra, popularly known as the "Theme from *2001,*" Elvis charged into the spotlight as though propelled by some supernatural force. He incoporated karate kicks and tai chi arabesques into his act as well as other dramatic postures. Elvis also mocked his 1950s sex-symbol image by exaggerating the pelvic thrusts and sexual posturings of his old performing style, while making jokes about the "old days." More peculiar parts of his act included wiping the sweat from his brow and throwing the scarf or towel into the audience. This gesture became such a popular ritual that dozens of white towels were kept just offstage so that Elvis could throw them into the audience at frequent intervals. The most curious ritual of all was not performed by Elvis, but by members of the audience. Each time Elvis played Las Vegas, the hotel stocked fresh undergarments in the restrooms because the women threw their underwear onto the stage while he was performing. Occasionally, they threw the keys to their hotel rooms.

Though Elvis's enormous popularity forced him to live a remote life secluded from

Above: Elvis's Vegas act evolved into a series of rituals and routines. Dramatic gestures were a part of his performing style. **Right:** The Colonel was never far away from his only client.

160

the public, his act onstage gave the illusion of intimacy. His rapport with his audiences was based on treating them like old friends or an extended family. Much interaction occurred onstage between Elvis and the audience members, such as the exchange of "gifts." Elvis threw towels and flowers into the audience; fans returned the gesture by throwing underwear, hotel keys, teddy bears, bouquets, and other mementos. Elvis kissed, hugged, and held hands with many of the women in the audience. They lined up just below the stage just like a receiving line for royalty, waiting to be blessed by the King's touch. Audience members expected Elvis to sing specific songs and perform familiar moves; he always fulfilled those expectations.

This type of interaction can be traced back to Elvis's early career, when audiences became hysterical at his gyrations and performing style. Even then, Elvis exhibited an uncanny instinct for knowing what the fans wanted to see and hear. He teased them with a few hip and leg movements, they responded, and then he cut loose, singling out specific members of the audience to interact with. This phenomenon was reciprocal in nature, forming a strong bond between performer and audience. If Elvis's fans were unusually loyal and demonstrative throughout his career, this interactive aspect of his act—from the beginning of his career to the end—was partially responsible.

If there is one symbol that has come to represent this period of Elvis's career, it is the bejeweled jumpsuits. As Elvis launched each new tour or Vegas appearance, his jumpsuits became more elaborate. Sometimes accompanied by a waist-length or floor-length cape,

Left, below, and below left: The International changed its name to the Las Vegas Hilton after Barron Hilton purchased it in 1971. Elvis performed at the hotel on 17 occasions, from 1969 through 1976.

Tailor Bill Belew designed many of Elvis's jumpsuits. Fans have named them according to their motifs: the Tiger or Mad Tiger (ABOVE), the Peacock (ABOVE RIGHT), and the Gypsy (RIGHT).

these costumes were decorated with real gems, jewels, and semiprecious stones. With the addition of chains and studs, these costumes could weigh as much as 30 pounds. Later costumes were emblazoned with certain symbols that had some symbolic significance to Elvis, including eagles, karate emblems, tigers, or sundials. Fans refer to these costumes by name—the Mexican Sundial, the King of Spades, the Rainbow Swirl, the American Eagle, the Red Flower, the Gypsy, and the Dragon—and they can identify specific tours and appearances by the costumes that Elvis wore.

Elvis's repertoire of songs varied after the early 1970s, but his style of music and the format of his act did not change. Fans like to find parallels between Elvis's personal life and the songs he chose to sing at certain points in his career. Around 1972, when Elvis and Priscilla were experiencing marital problems, he included "Always on My Mind" and "You Gave Me a Mountain," two songs about the trials and tribulations of life and love. The following year, Elvis included "My Way" in his act. Paul Anka wrote the lyrics for this powerful song, which are about a man reflecting back on his life as death draws near, with Frank Sinatra in mind. Yet, the song became a personal anthem for Elvis—one that seemed to explain his eccentric lifestyle and larger-than-life image. A single release of this song by Elvis was not distributed until June of 1977—two months before he died.

In 1971, country songwriter Mickey Newbury put together a unique arrangement of three 19th-century songs, which he record-ed and released as "An American Trilogy." Elvis heard the record and immediately incorporated "An American Trilogy" into his act. The piece has become so associated with Elvis Presley that it is difficult to imagine anyone else performing it with the same showstopping fervor that Elvis always did. A combination of "Dixie," "The Battle Hymn of the Republic," and the spiritual "All My Trials," the medley reflects Elvis's patriotism, his religious convictions, and his deep affection for his native South.

A Vegas-style comedian always opened Elvis's concerts, even when he was on the road. Rock music aficionados were appalled by the old-fashioned routines and stale jokes of these stand-up comics, particularly because this era saw the rise of a new, more hip generation of comedians with socially relevant material. But, even when he was on the cutting edge of rock 'n' roll in 1956 and 1957, Elvis always toured with an oddball assortment of vaudeville-flavored acts dug up by the Colonel. It seems only natural that the Colonel would hire this type of opening act when Elvis returned to live performances in the 1970s. Elvis and the Colonel were accustomed to this kind of show business act, and the humor went over well in Vegas. Sammy Shore opened for Elvis in the early 1970s, while Jackie Kahane did the honors after 1972.

Kahane's responsibilities included announcing, "Ladies and gentlemen, Elvis has left the building," at the end of each performance. Elvis rarely performed an encore, though many times the audience remained behind after the final number hoping Elvis

Comedian Jackie Kahane often opened for Elvis. During Elvis's performances, the female vocal trio the Sweet Inspirations sang backup as did J.D. Sumner and the Stamps Quartet.

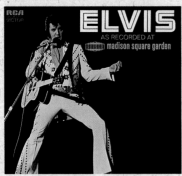

Top: At the press conference for Elvis's appearance at Madison Square Garden, reporters teased the flamboyant singer about his powder blue suit with matching cape. **Above and right:** Elvis's performance at the Garden on June 10, 1972, was recorded and made into an album. The album achieved gold-record status by August 4 of that year.

would respond to the thunderous applause and return for one last song. To avoid any problems with overzealous fans, Elvis always ran backstage immediately after the last song, often while the band was still playing, and dashed into a car waiting at the stage door. Kahane's announcement let the audience know that it was truly time to leave.

Despite the lack of change in Elvis's live performances during the 1970s, there are still many highlights. In June 1972, Elvis played Madison Square Garden in New York City. This was the first time he'd ever played live in New York. All four shows at the Garden quickly sold out, but Elvis and his management team were afraid that the sophisticated New York critics wouldn't like his Las Vegas-style show. Elvis was decked out in one of his bejeweled jumpsuits on opening night. The outfit included a gold-lined cape and a gigantic belt emblazoned with "The World Champion Entertainer"—just in case the critics didn't know who they were dealing with. Throughout the show, particularly while he was singing his old songs, Elvis maintained an ironic distance from his audience. Sometimes he couldn't resist joking about his former image. At the beginning of "Hound Dog," for example, Elvis dropped dramatically down to one knee, and then said, "Oh, excuse me," before switching to the other knee.

During the engagement in New York, Elvis appeared to be in top physical condition. His voice was strong and clear, and he sang a variety of old and new songs with drama and flair. Most of the New York critics were enthusiastic. RCA recorded all four shows at the Garden for an album titled *Elvis as Recorded at Madison Square Garden*. The songs were mixed, the records were pressed, and the albums were in the stores in less than two weeks.

MGM produced and released two documentaries that captured Elvis's live performances. *Elvis—That's the Way It Is* is a feature-length movie built around Elvis's August 1970 engagement at the International in Las Vegas. About half of the movie features his performance on stage in the main room. One segment in which Elvis sings "Mystery Train" and "Tiger Man" was filmed at a concert in Phoenix. The rest of the movie documents the excitement Elvis generated as a performer. Elvis is shown in rehearsal for the show, whipping his band into shape and mastering new material for the act. Intercut with the rehearsal footage are shots of the massive promotional buildup in Las Vegas. A film crew was also sent to Luxembourg to record an Elvis Presley convention.

Elvis—That's the Way It Is was directed by Denis Sanders, who won an Oscar for Best Documentary for his film *Czechoslovakia 1968*. Expert cinematographer Lucien Ballard caught the excitement of Elvis's performance on stage with eight Panavision cameras. The film was released on November 11, 1970, to good reviews. The *Hollywood Reporter*

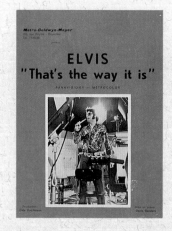

Above, left, and below left: The documentary *Elvis—That's the Way It Is* chronicled the King's 1970 summer appearance at the International. The film is structured so that rehearsals and other scenes of preparation build to an extended climax of Elvis onstage. Several show-business luminaries attended the performance at the International. A wide range of celebrities—from bandleader Xaviar Cugat and wife Charro to dancer Juliet Prowse to actor Dale Robertson—were captured on film by the camera crew as they entered the main showroom.

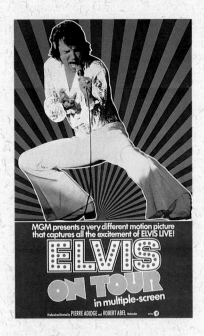

Above and right: The second documentary to capture Elvis in performance, *Elvis on Tour*, focused on his road show.

remarked that Elvis was probably the only entertainer alive who could draw enough people into a theater to make a documentary profitable at the box office. The film also introduced Elvis as a live performer to an audience who was too young to remember him from the 1950s and knew Elvis only from his movies.

In 1972, MGM released another feature-length documentary about Elvis, which had been shot in the spring of that year. *Elvis on Tour* focuses on his road show during a 15-city tour. This film captures the final phase of Elvis's career at its highest point. It was produced by Pierre Adidge and Robert Abel, who

had won critical acclaim for their rock documentary *Joe Cocker: Mad Dogs and Englishmen*. Some of the editing was supervised by Martin Scorsese, who also worked on the editing of *Woodstock*. Andrew Solt is credited with doing research on *Elvis on Tour*. He later coproduced the semidocumentary *This Is Elvis* as well as *Imagine*, a film about John Lennon. *Elvis on Tour* won a Golden Globe for the Best Documentary of 1972; it is the only Elvis Presley movie to be honored with an award of any kind.

In January 1973, Elvis returned to television with a spectacular special, *Elvis: Aloha from Hawaii*. The show was a benefit for cancer research, and all the proceeds from the concert went to the Kui Lee Cancer Fund of Hawaii. Elvis's performance at the Honolulu International Center Arena was broadcast live via the Intelsat IV telecommunications satellite to Japan, Korea, the Philippines, New Zealand, Australia, Thailand, South Vietnam, and other countries in the Far East. Two days later, a taped replay was aired in Western Europe, and in April, the special was rebroadcast on American television. Over one and a half billion people eventually watched this one performance. Dressed in a trademark jumpsuit with matching cape, Elvis sang both new material and his well-known hit songs. By the end of the show, he was so caught up in the enthusiasm of the audience and in the magnitude of the event that he hurled his cape, which was worth several thousand dollars, into the audience.

The years 1969 through 1973 were an incredibly creative time for Elvis. He returned to performing live and developed a new sound and a new image that completely replaced the singing-movie-star image that he believed never really matched his talents. Dressed in gold and jewels, this Elvis Presley lived up to the titles "World's Greatest Entertainer" and "The King of Rock 'n' Roll."

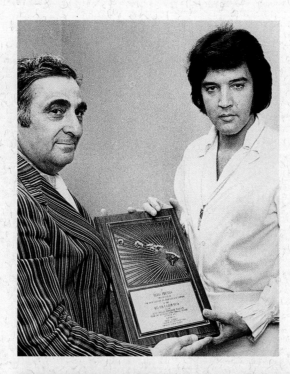

Left and below: Though televised around the world, *Elvis: Aloha from Hawaii* was actually a benefit concert for the Kui Lee Cancer Fund, which was based in Hawaii. The singer received a plaque from the organization for his efforts in making the concert a success.

Above: The soundtrack to Elvis's TV special was a two-record set that was certified gold within a month of release. **Above right:** Elvis arrived in Honolulu on January 9, 1973, amidst a flock of fans. **Below right and opposite page:** On January 14, *Elvis: Aloha from Hawaii* was beamed to several countries around the world via the Intelsat IV communications satellite.

CHAPTER NINE

THE KING IS DEAD

"THE KING IS ALWAYS KILLED BY HIS COURTIERS.
HE IS OVERFED, OVERINDULGED, OVERDRUNK TO KEEP HIM TIED
TO HIS THRONE. MOST PEOPLE IN THE POSITION NEVER WAKE UP."

—John Lennon, on the death of Elvis Presley

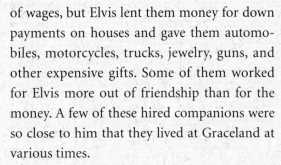

When talking about Elvis Presley, the King of Rock 'n' Roll, it is almost impossible to ignore the analogy of royalty. He was adored by his fans, he was enormously wealthy, and he dressed in jewels and flowing capes. Elvis enjoyed many of the privileges and pleasures fit for a king; even his eccentric and secluded lifestyle was indicative of the spoils of royalty.

Like all kings, Elvis had his court. The entertainment press called this group of close friends, business associates, and employees "the Memphis Mafia." They not only worked for Elvis, but also kept him entertained. Elvis, the Colonel, and Vernon Presley never paid the members of the Mafia very much in terms of wages, but Elvis lent them money for down payments on houses and gave them automobiles, motorcycles, trucks, jewelry, guns, and other expensive gifts. Some of them worked for Elvis more out of friendship than for the money. A few of these hired companions were so close to him that they lived at Graceland at various times.

Over the years, the faces in the group changed, but a few men remained with Elvis for much of his career. The most prominent members of the court include Red and Sonny West (who were cousins), Marty Lacker, Joe Esposito, George Klein, Jerry Schilling, Charlie Hodge, Gene Smith (Elvis's cousin), Lamar Fike, and Alan Fortas. Some members of the Memphis Mafia didn't work for Elvis exclusively but had their own careers. George Klein worked as a disc jockey in and around Memphis for most of his life. Red West, who had been with Elvis since about 1955, worked as a stuntman in Hollywood. In addition to doing stunt work in most of Elvis's movies, he worked in the film *Spartacus* and in several television series. West also wrote songs for Elvis and other singers, including Ricky Nelson, Pat Boone, and Johnny Rivers.

Elvis and his court even had their own coat of arms. A lightning bolt combined with the initials TCB was designed by Elvis to symbolize the code of honor that he wanted his entourage to live by. TCB stood for "taking care of business," while the lightning bolt represented speed, so the insignia meant "taking care of business in a flash." Elvis liked everything to be done quickly and efficiently. Elvis had charms made up with this insignia for

Red West, Elvis's friend and bodyguard for many years, often appeared in bit roles in Elvis's films. In *Clambake*, Red appeared as an ice-cream vendor (FAR RIGHT) in a musical production number.

Elvis served as best man and Priscilla was maid of honor at Sonny West's wedding to Judy Morgan in December 1971.

The "TCB" on Elvis's karate robe represented a code of honor he wanted his entourage to live by. TCB meant "taking care of business," while the lightning bolt signified speed.

On the set of *Follow That Dream* in Florida, Elvis takes a break with some of his friends. Members of the Memphis Mafia, his entourage of buddy-bodyguards, accompanied him wherever he went.

each member of the Memphis Mafia, and many of the men wore them on chains around their necks. Later, Elvis had TLC charms—signifying "tender, loving care"—custom-made for the wives and girlfriends of those closest to him.

During the 1960s, members of the Memphis Mafia joined Elvis on location while he was making movies. Some of the men had bit parts, but their main job was to keep Elvis company. When he was shooting a movie at a studio in Hollywood, Elvis and his entourage lived in a Bel Air mansion that had once belonged to the Shah of Iran. The house was

the scene of many late-night parties, which were often attended by a host of Hollywood starlets.

As Elvis grew bored with making movies, his antics and practical jokes got wilder and more elaborate. At first the tedium of movie production was relieved by a football team Elvis organized in Hollywood to pass the time in a constructive manner. Several young actors participated in these games, including Kent McCord, Ty Hardin, Pat Boone, Robert Conrad, Gary Lockwood, and Ricky Nelson. As time went on, Elvis took up more expensive hobbies to fill his time while in Holly-

Football was Elvis's favorite sport. In the early 1960s, he organized his friends into teams and often hired referees to officiate the games. While in Hollywood, Elvis organized several young actors into a loose-knit team to play football on Sundays.

The Elvis Presley Enterprises was a Memphis football team that Elvis sponsored in the fall of 1963. Occasionally, Elvis played with the Enterprises.

As Elvis grew bored with his movie career, he and the Memphis Mafia increased their antics on the set during production. Memos from studio officials were issued requesting that the group tone down their practical jokes and high jinks.

wood. On one shopping spree during the production of *Tickle Me*, Elvis bought all of his friends motorbikes so they could go riding together.

While on the set, Elvis and his friends pulled practical jokes on members of the cast and crew. After Elvis lost respect for his movies, his quest for fun tended to take precedence over his acting. Even pie fights were not uncommon. On the set of *Easy Come, Easy Go*, Elvis and director John Rich bickered over the constant mayhem and foolishness that ensued. During one scene, Elvis kept breaking into laughter every time he looked at Red or Sonny West, causing him to blow his lines in take after take. Rich lost his temper and

ordered everyone off the set, but Elvis stepped in and set Rich straight. "We're doing these movies because it's supposed to be fun, nothing more," he told his director. "When they cease to be fun, then we'll cease to do them." Later, the group caused so much confusion during the filming of *Clambake* that when production on *Stay Away, Joe* began, a memo came down from the MGM executive offices warning Elvis and the Memphis Mafia about their behavior.

When Elvis wasn't working on a movie, he and his buddy-bodyguards retreated behind the gates of Graceland. Occasionally, they ventured out into Memphis to seek entertainment. Since Elvis's persistent fans prevented him from going out during normal hours, he often rented the Malco or the Memphian movie theaters from midnight to dawn. Elvis, his friends, and their guests would stay up all night watching the latest movies as well as older films. Before the midnight movies at the Malco became his passion, Elvis often rented amusement parks or roller skating rinks after hours for the entertainment of his friends.

When Elvis first became a national singing sensation, he enjoyed the adoring fans who followed him around or waited for him in front of his house. On his first visit to Hollywood, Elvis and his buddies cruised up and down Hollywood Boulevard, inciting his fans to follow their car. They'd pull up to a stoplight, and Elvis would roll down his car window, take off his sunglasses, and yell to the girls standing on the corner. When the light changed, Elvis and company would take off

Because of overzealous fans, Elvis felt he had to seclude himself at Graceland, which made for an unusual, isolated existence.

179

again, leaving a crowd of people screaming hysterically in the middle of the intersection or chasing their car down the street.

As time passed, the fans became too much for him to manage. He was mobbed, pushed down, and sometimes stripped bare by crowds of adoring admirers. Elvis couldn't sightsee, eat in a restaurant, or enjoy himself in public without his fans besieging him. By the time Elvis was discharged from the army, he had begun living as a recluse. He secluded himself at Graceland or his home in California. This isolation, coupled with his boredom when he was between projects, eventually led Elvis to indulge in several destructive habits.

These bad habits accelerated during the 1970s after he returned to performing in concert and a hectic life on the road. His worst problem was obviously his dependence on prescription drugs, which altered his behavior and personality. According to members of the Memphis Mafia, Elvis began using amphetamines and diet pills in the 1960s; the drugs were intended to help Elvis keep his weight down. To counteract the amphetamines, Elvis and his court, who always indulged in whatever Elvis was doing, began to take sleeping pills. By the early 1970s, when he was touring on a debilitating schedule of one-nighters, Elvis was taking medication for pain and discomfort caused by various afflictions and conditions. These drugs eventually left him in a state of mental limbo. Members of the Memphis Mafia disagree about how many drugs Elvis took, but the fact remains that he took more drugs than his body could withstand. His drug abuse not only brought on a decline in his career but it also led to his death.

Elvis's drug problem was the result of prescription drugs, some of which were administered for health problems. He had back pain, digestive troubles, and many eye afflictions, including glaucoma. Treatments for these conditions put Elvis in the hospital several times between 1973 and his death four years later. He was also hospitalized for throat ailments, pleurisy, and hypertension. Ironically, Elvis rarely indulged in alcohol and often spoke out against taking illegal drugs.

Because of his wealth and position, Elvis indulged in certain excesses that have been so exaggerated that they are now a part of his legend. Particularly outrageous statements have been made about Elvis's eating habits and choice of foods. He was a lifelong fan of junk food and Southern-style cooking. As

By the mid-1970s, Elvis's performances were sometimes peppered with exaggerated stage mannerisms indicative of drug-influenced behavior.

In the last couple years of his life, Elvis looked unhealthy, largely due to a massive weight gain.

early as 1955, when he was still considered an up-and-coming country-western singer, articles about the young entertainer often mentioned that he liked to down several cheeseburgers at one sitting. An article in *Esquire* magazine in the late 1960s took a sarcastic but lighthearted tone when describing Elvis's favorite snack of peanut butter and mashed banana sandwiches washed down with several Pepsis. After Elvis's death, this kind of report on his eating habits took on a sinister connotation. The stories were sometimes used to suggest that Elvis was out of control and that his eating habits and weight problems were somehow related to his drug abuse. These attempts at armchair psychology don't take into account the fact that Elvis always had these eating habits and that age and lack of exercise had as much to do with his weight gain as anything else.

Most of Elvis's favorite foods were typical Southern dishes, which incorporate a variety of fried meats. Reporters and magazine writers who were not familiar with Southern cooking felt that Elvis's eating habits were peculiar, although many people in the South enjoy the same foods Elvis liked to eat. Other writers reported that the amount of food Elvis consumed was excessive. They told tall tales about Elvis eating so many Spanish omelettes that he created an egg shortage in Tennessee. Another story claims Elvis once ate 30 cups of yogurt, eight honeydew melons, and a hundred dollars' worth of ice cream bars in one night. Elvis sometimes went on eating binges, particularly during his time off between projects, but the stories about his binges on such foods as bacon, ice cream, cheeseburgers, and pizza have been repeated so often that they suggest that Elvis ate this much every day. It's as though Elvis's larger-than-life image, particularly during the last phase of his career, required tall tales of eating feats to support his legendary status.

Not all of Elvis's excesses were bad for his health. He also liked to collect and wear ostentatious jewelry, which is perhaps an extravagance more befitting a "king." During the 1970s, Elvis wore rings on all his fingers both on stage and off. He also wore heavy medallions, gold-plated belts, and chain-link bracelets. On a gold chain around his neck, Elvis wore a gold Star of David as well as a

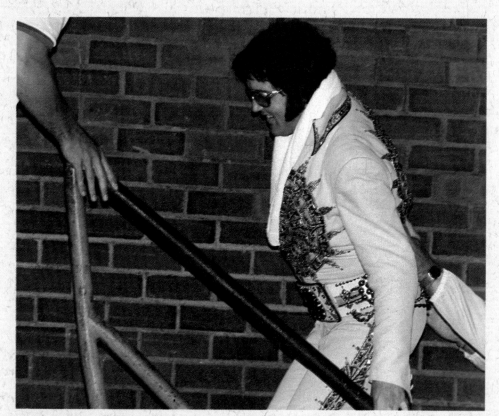

Elvis had some of his jumpsuits altered to accommodate the extra pounds.

Elvis's extravagances included his tendency to bestow expensive gifts not only on his friends but also to people he admired. A longtime fan of Muhammed Ali, Elvis once gave the fighter a robe valued at more than $10,000.

crucifix. He also liked to carry walking sticks adorned with tops made of silver or gold. Elvis bought expensive jewelry not only for himself but also for the Memphis Mafia, their wives, and his show business friends. He once gave Sammy Davis, Jr., a $30,000 ring.

Elvis had a lifelong love affair with Cadillacs and bought more than 100 during the course of his career, mostly for himself and the members of his entourage. One of the first cars Elvis purchased was a 1956 pink Cadillac sedan. He promptly gave the car to his mother, Gladys, despite the fact that she couldn't drive. This was the only Cadillac that Elvis kept throughout his life, and it is still owned by the Elvis Presley estate. In addition to Cadillacs, Elvis bought unique foreign cars such as a three-door Messerschmidt as well as more prestigious automobiles, including a Mercedes limousine and a Rolls-Royce. Elvis's most outrageous vehicle was his 1960 Cadillac limousine that had been customized by George Barris. It was painted with diamond-dust gold paint and featured a motorized shoe-shine kit, a wet bar, a television, and a record player. The car was too cumbersome and impractical to use every day, so Elvis lent the gold Cadillac to MGM to promote one of his movies. The car is now on display in the Country Music Hall of Fame in Nashville.

Elvis was infatuated with law enforcement and collected police badges from across the country. Elvis asked the sheriff of Shelby County, Tennessee, to give him, his father, his doctor, and most members of the Memphis Mafia deputy's badges. Elvis also had a badge from the Palm Springs Police Department, and he had close friends who were members of the Los Angeles Police Department and the Denver Police. Considering that Elvis was once regarded as a rebel who opposed authority, it's ironic that he had so much respect for law-enforcement officials.

In December 1970, Elvis made a spontaneous decision to travel to Washington, D.C., to visit Deputy U.S. Narcotics Director John Finlator. Although Elvis said that he was going to Washington to volunteer his help in the antidrug campaign, he was really hoping to obtain a federal narcotics badge and a complete set of credentials to add to his collection. Director Finlator turned down Elvis's request for a badge, but this did not stop Elvis. He decided to go over Finlator's head, and with a couple of members of the Memphis Mafia, Elvis called on President Richard Nixon at the White House. The charismatic Presley was able to talk Nixon into giving him an authentic narcotics agent's badge in a matter of minutes. He then asked the President to track down some souvenirs inscribed with the presidential seal for his bodyguards and their wives. On later trips to Washington, Elvis visited FBI headquarters to offer his assistance in fighting the war on drugs. While it's not surprising that Elvis visited law-enforcement agencies, the fact that he could get in to see the president on a few hours' notice is extraordinary testimony to Elvis's amazing popularity and power. Other entertainers have been honored to be invited to perform at the White House, but Elvis simply dropped in to get something he wanted.

Opposite page: Elvis often purchased cars for himself and others on the slightest whim. Here he takes possession of his third Stutz Bearcat.

Elvis was infatuated with law enforcement most of his life. **Above:** The entire entourage, including Dr. George Nichopolous (TO ELVIS'S LEFT), show off their deputy's badges from Shelby County, Tennessee. **Opposite page:** Elvis met President Richard Nixon when he went to Washington, D.C., to obtain a federal narcotics agent's badge.

Elvis also collected guns and other kinds of weapons. He owned thousands of dollars worth of guns, but Elvis was especially fond of a huge .44 magnum, a little Derringer similar to those carried by nineteenth-century riverboat gamblers, a turquoise-handled Colt .45, and a pearl-handled undercover .38. Elvis also lavished expensive guns on the members of the Memphis Mafia. His bodyguards, particularly Red and Sonny West, often carried their weapons on them and so did Elvis. When Elvis boarded a commercial flight on his way to see President Nixon, he was packing a pistol. When the ticket agent followed him onto the plane to tell him he couldn't take a gun on board, Elvis left the plane in a huff. The pilot came scurrying after him, apologized for the ticket agent, and allowed Elvis to get back on the airplane.

During the 1970s, Elvis carried a gun with him much of the time, partly because he was concerned for his safety. After he returned to performing before live audiences, Elvis received many death and kidnapping threats. He believed that assassins sought glory or media attention when they attempted to kill a famous person, and they were so eager for fame that they were willing to chance death or living out their lives in prison to attain recognition. In 1971, while Elvis was performing in Las Vegas, an anonymous caller got through to his hotel room and warned him that there would be an assassination attempt during that evening's performance. Later that day, Elvis received a menu from the International Hotel with his picture on the front. The picture had been defaced, and a handgun had been drawn near Elvis's heart. A message included with the menu read, "Guess who, and where?" The FBI was called in, which must have both thrilled and frightened Elvis, and the hotel management told him he did not have to go on. But Elvis stuck a Derringer into his boot and a .45 into his belt, and he did the show anyway.

During another incident in Las Vegas in 1973, four drunks suddenly bolted onto the stage during Elvis's midnight show. Red West subdued one of the men, and three members of the Memphis Mafia, Vernon Presley, and one of the Colonel's assistants scuffled with two others and eventually drug them offstage. Elvis knocked the fourth man off the stage himself and sent him hurtling into the crowd. Then Elvis apologized to the audience, telling them he was sorry; that is, he was sorry he didn't break the man's neck. The statement brought down the house; there was a seven-minute standing ovation from the crowd.

Opposite page: Elvis asked Nixon to track down some White House souvenirs for friends Jerry Schiller and Sonny West as well as for their wives. **Far left:** When Deputy U.S. Narcotics Director John Finlator refused to give Elvis a federal agent's badge, Elvis went over his head and got one through Nixon.

that his talent and success came from God. He felt strongly that if he didn't extend some of his good fortune to other people, it could all be taken away from him. Throughout his career, Elvis recorded gospel albums that featured his favorite hymns. (Elvis won three Grammy Awards during his career—all for gospel albums.) During the 1960s, actress Donna Douglas and several other friends encouraged Elvis to expand his religious beliefs by reading about theology and religion. Later, Elvis's long time hairdresser Larry Geller inspired Elvis to read books on the occult, esoteric healing, and Eastern religions.

Elvis became deeply involved with his reading and spent many evenings attempting to discuss what he had read with his entourage and their female companions, who had a difficult time keeping up with Elvis's lofty pursuits. During the time he was reading esoteric religious books, he became so deeply involved in his studies that his personality began to change. Rumors maintain that at one point, Elvis decided he had special spiritual powers that allowed him to heal the sick and commune with nature. Everyone around him became concerned, until Colonel Parker finally stepped in and persuaded Elvis that Larry Geller was an unhealthy influence. Elvis accepted Parker's advice; he dropped Geller from his group of friends and tempered his interest in spiritual topics.

The King may have had his faults and his eccentricities, but he was regally generous. Elvis not only gave freely to his friends and their families but he also donated large amounts of money to charity and organized benefit concerts. Tales about his generosity to

Bodyguards Sonny West (TOP) and Red West (BOTTOM) were cautious about letting strangers near Elvis after the singer received death threats in the mid-1970s. However, they were criticized for their brutal tactics.

Over the next few years, there were so many death threats and other incidents that bodyguards Red and Sonny West became cautious about allowing strangers to get near Elvis. Their tactics were often rough, and they were frequently criticized by other entertainers and people in the industry. At least three lawsuits were filed against Elvis in conjunction with the strong-arm tactics of his guards. Elvis himself is said to have saved his violent aggression for television sets. He had a reputation for shooting the TV when something came on that he didn't want to see. The number of times he actually shot out televisions has probably been exaggerated much like the stories about Elvis's eating binges, but he was known to have blasted a few television sets with the Derringer he kept in his boot.

Despite his excessive lifestyle, Elvis was deeply interested in religious philosophy and spiritual thought. His behavior may not have always matched his beliefs, but Elvis believed complete strangers have become part of his legend. Once, while he was buying a couple of El Dorados for members of his entourage, Elvis noticed a young couple who were wandering around the dealer's lot, trying to find a car that they could afford. Elvis told them to pick any car they wanted, then he wrote out a check and left the salesman to do the paperwork. Another time, he gave away seven Cadillacs and Lincolns to people in Colorado. This inspired a local radio newscaster to joke on the air that he wouldn't mind having a little sports car. The next day a Cadillac Seville was delivered to the newsman. A Seville is hardly a sports car, but the man wasn't going to complain.

Above: Elvis bought a car for stranger Mennie Person (RIGHT) simply because she admired his limousine. Mrs. Person's daughter, Benita, is shown leaning against her mom's new car. **Left:** Elvis makes another car salesman happy.

Elvis was also generous in less flamboyant ways. On the flight to Washington, D.C., to see the president, Elvis noticed a soldier who was returning home for the Christmas holidays. Knowing firsthand how little money servicemen are paid, Elvis told his travelling companions to give the soldier all of their cash. They gave him about $500, which meant that Elvis and his friends had to rely on their credit cards to pay for the rest of their trip. Another time, Elvis gave $500 to a blind man who was selling pencils. When he read in the paper about a poverty-stricken black woman in dire need of a wheelchair, Elvis bought her a motorized chair and delivered it himself. Many times, when he saw a news report about a police officer who had been killed, Elvis called the television station to get the name of the officer's widow so that he could send her money. Every Christmas, Elvis and Vernon donated $1,000 checks to at least 100 Memphis charities. Few entertainers could match Elvis for his generosity.

A life of isolation from the outside world combined with the privileges of stardom eventually led Elvis to self-destruct. He led a secluded existence inside the walls of Graceland, where there was no one with enough influence to stop the indulgences of the King. Still, Elvis's dark habits and self-destructive whims are often exaggerated to such a degree that only a fantasy figure could have indulged in proportions of this magnitude. Perhaps normal standards of measurement are simply not adequate when describing the excesses and achievements of Elvis Presley. For all his monstrosity and for all of the heartbreaking details that have been revealed since his death, the one part of the legend that remains untarnished is his voice— which rang true and clear from the day he recorded "That's All Right" until June 26, 1977, the day he gave his final performance in Market Square Arena in Indianapolis.

Elvis Presley died at Graceland on August 16, 1977. He was 42 years old. Girlfriend Ginger Alden found him slumped over in the bathroom. Paramedics were called, but they failed to revive Elvis, and he was taken to Baptist Memorial Hospital where further attempts to resuscitate him failed. He was pronounced dead by his physician, Dr. George Nichopolous, who listed the official cause of death as erratic heartbeat (cardiac arrhythmia).

Almost immediately, rumors that Elvis was dead began to sift into Memphis newspaper offices and radio and television newsrooms, but reporters took a wait-and-see atti-

Elvis often donated money to the wives of police officers killed in the line of duty. Police all over the country respected Elvis for his generosity.

tude. Many of them had heard these rumors before. Over the years, many crank calls had come into the newsroom declaring that Elvis had been killed in a car accident or a plane crash, or that he'd been shot by the jealous boyfriend of a woman who was hopelessly infatuated with him. Once, someone reported that he had drowned in a submarine. Elvis Presley was a hometown boy and a constant source of news, some of which was manufactured for or by the Memphis press. Newspaper editors and newsroom managers were cautious about sending out their reporters if the rumor that Elvis was dead was just another hoax. But when the staff of the *Memphis Press-Scimitar* learned from a trusted source that Elvis actually was dead, the newsroom became unusually silent. Dan Sears of radio station WMPS in Memphis made the first official announcement, and WHBQ-TV was the first television station to interrupt its programming with the terrible news.

As the news of Elvis's death spread across the country, radio stations immediately began to play his records. Some stations quickly organized tributes to Elvis while others simply played his music at the request of listeners, many of whom were in a state of shock by the announcement of his sudden death. Some people called their favorite radio stations just because they wanted to tell someone their stories about the first time they'd heard Elvis sing or to talk about how much his talent and his music had meant to them. In the same way that many people remember exactly where they were when they heard that President John F. Kennedy had been killed, most of Elvis's fans remember where they were the day Elvis died. Mick Fleetwood of the rock group Fleetwood Mac recalls, "The news came over like a ton of bricks. I was driving back from the mountains and I had the radio on. They were playing an Elvis medley and I thought, 'Great.' And then they came back with the news."

The manner in which the major television networks handled the news of Elvis's death illustrated his enormous popularity and the tremendous impact he had on America, something few realized until he was gone. Data from the television-ratings service Arbitron revealed that on the day Elvis died, there was a huge increase in the number of televisions tuned to evening news programs. The staffs of television newsrooms considered Elvis's death a late-breaking story. There was not enough time for TV reporters who had been sent to Memphis to file stories for the evening news. Executives had to decide quickly what film footage they could use from their files and

Above: The Memphis papers announce the grim news of Elvis's death. **Far left:** Elvis's last girlfriend, Ginger Alden, discovered his lifeless body. Paramedics were called, but they failed to revive him.

Above: After Elvis died, many fans with tickets to his scheduled concerts decided to hold onto them as souvenirs. **Right:** Local merchants pay their respects to Memphis's favorite native son.

where to place the story in relation to the other news of the day.

NBC-TV not only rewrote their news line-up to lead off with the story of Elvis's death, but the network also made immediate plans to delay *The Tonight Show* and put together a late-night news documentary. David Brinkley was a national news anchor for NBC at that time, and he opened his broadcast with three minutes devoted to Elvis's sudden death. ABC-TV also decided to lead off with the Presley story. When they learned that NBC would be doing a late-night news special about the significance of Elvis Presley to American music, ABC announced that they would also air a half-hour documentary.

The *CBS Evening News with Walter Cronkite* had led the ratings in news programming for more than a decade. The lure of the program was Cronkite, the most respected man in broadcasting at that time. CBS executives decided not to open their evening broadcast with the Presley story. Arbitron's records indicate that when millions of viewers realized this, they immediately switched to another network. The CBS decision not to lead with Elvis's death gave the *CBS Evening News* its lowest ratings in years. (For the record, Roger Mudd was substituting for Walter Cronkite that evening.) CBS devoted only 70 seconds to their story on Elvis, putting it after a lengthy segment on the Panama Canal. The producer for that evening's news was vehemently opposed to leading off with Elvis's death, even though other members of the CBS programming staff suggested it repeatedly. Interviewed later, the producer agreed that he was out of sync with the national consciousness. Two days later, CBS tried to save face by putting together a documentary on Elvis.

Even though Elvis never performed in Europe, countries from all over the world sent reporters to Memphis. Press coverage in foreign newspapers and on European television was almost as extensive as reporting in the United States. Everywhere in the world, people lamented the loss of an irreplaceable entertainer.

Within an hour after Elvis's death, fans began to gather in front of Graceland. By the next day, when the gates were opened for mourners to view Elvis's body, the crowd was estimated at about 20,000. By the time the gates closed at 6:30 P.M., about 80,000 fans passed by Elvis's coffin. Many had come from different parts of the country; many from different parts of the world. Eventually, so many mourners arrived that it was impossible for all of them to be admitted to Graceland, even with extended calling hours. Law enforcement officials were afraid that there might be problems with crowd control, but only one unfortunate incident occurred. A drunk driver careened into three teenagers, killing two of them.

As the group of mourners around the gates of Graceland grew, a carnival atmosphere developed; people hawking T-shirts and other souvenirs began to work the crowd. The people who were unable to get into Graceland to pay their last respects to Elvis consoled each other by exchanging anecdotes about their idol. When reporters asked them why they were there, people inevitably gave the same reply: They didn't really know, but they felt they wanted to be where he was this one last time. The hot Memphis weather and the close crush of the crowd caused many people to pass out. A medic was stationed nearby to assist anyone who fainted, but no one left because of the heat.

Elvis's fans sent a tremendous array of flowers, which were set out along the bank in front of the house. Every blossom in Memphis had been sold by the afternoon of August 17, and additional flowers were shipped in from other parts of the country. It was the biggest day in the history of FTD, a florists' delivery service. FTD employees claim that more 2,150 arrangements were delivered. The arrangements were shaped like lightning bolts, gui-

Top and bottom: Within an hour after the announcement of Elvis's death, mourners began to gather at Graceland. Many stayed until after his funeral.

Opposite page top: By the funeral, on August 18, 1977, the line of mourners at Graceland extended past the estate and around the block. **Opposite page bottom:** A police woman pays her respects as the hearse passes through the Music Gates. **Above and above left:** As mourners watched, the long motor cortege of all-white automobiles headed toward Forest Hill Cemetery. **Left:** Official pallbearers included Joe Esposito, Dr. George Nichopolous, Billy Smith, Charlie Hodge, and Lamar Fike.

Right: A saddened Sam Phillips pays his last respects to his most famous discovery. **Below right:** Ann-Margret and husband Roger Smith were among several celebrities who attended Elvis's funeral.

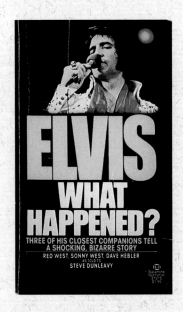

and their vocal groups, as well as singer Kathy Westmoreland, sang. The casket was carried to Forest Hill Cemetery in a long motor cortege of all-white automobiles. Later, after someone threatened to steal Elvis's remains, his casket was moved to Meditation Gardens behind Graceland. Gladys's body was moved to Meditation Gardens in 1977; Vernon Presley died and was buried there in 1979; and Minnie Mae Presley was laid to rest beside the rest of her family in 1980.

Just 15 days before Elvis died, on August 1, 1977, Ballantine Books published a book put together by Steve Dunleavy. It consisted of interviews with three of Elvis's former body-guards, Red West, Sonny West, and Dave Hebler. The three men were the first to come forward with stories of Elvis's bizarre lifestyle. *Elvis: What Happened?* included accounts of his mood swings, his relationships with women, and his excessive use of prescription drugs. The book received almost no publicity until journalist Bob Greene, a columnist for the *Chicago Sun-Times*, interviewed Sonny West for his syndicated column. By coinci-dence, the article happened to run on the day that Elvis died. Greene's column provoked a great deal of protest from fans across the country and inspired the wrath of several journalists, including Geraldo Rivera, who blasted Dunleavy on *Good Morning America* for smearing Elvis's name.

The bodyguards' story was difficult to believe for several reasons. Nothing like it had surfaced on a wide scale before, because for the most part, Elvis had been able to keep his eccentric habits and erratic behavior out of the press. Dunleavy also lacked credibility. He

Far left: Fans express their grief at Elvis's crypt. The bodies of both Elvis and Gladys were moved to Meditation Gardens at Graceland in October 1977.
Above: *Elvis: What Happened?*, which revealed Elvis's self-destructive lifestyle and drug misuse, was published just a cou-ple of weeks before Elvis died.

tars, hound dogs, and stars, as well as more traditional wreaths and bouquets. Many of the arrangements were sent immediately to Forest Hill Cemetery, the site of the burial, where they shared space with more humble arrange-ments of daisies in coke bottles. After the funeral, Vernon allowed the fans to take away the flowers as souvenirs.

Many celebrities attended Elvis's funeral, including Caroline Kennedy, country music guitarist Chet Atkins, performers Ann-Margret and George Hamilton, and television evangelist Rex Humbard, who was one of the speakers during the service. Comedian Jackie Kahane, who had opened many of Elvis's con-cert performances, delivered his eulogy, and a local minister also spoke. Gospel performers Jake Hess, J.D. Sumner, and James Blackwood, had been a reporter for the tabloid newspaper the *National Enquirer* when he started working on the book about Elvis, and he was employed by the controversial newspaper the *New York Post* when *Elvis: What Happened?* was published. Dunleavy also appeared on the NBC documentary about Elvis that aired on the evening he died. Dunleavy made the mistake of using the term "white trash" in reference to Elvis, and this didn't go over very well with the fans. Since Dunleavy wasn't popular with either the public or the press and because Vernon had fired the three bodyguards the previous year, many people believed that their outrageous account of Elvis's life was just sour grapes over being dismissed. Dunleavy was accused of having manipulated the story to make it as sensational as possible.

Over the next two years, reports of Elvis's drug abuse and its relationship to his death surfaced occasionally, but little was done about it. Interestingly, it was Geraldo Rivera who helped uncover the truth about Elvis's drug misuse. In 1979, Rivera and Charles Thompson, a producer for the television news magazine *20/20*, obtained a copy of a confidential report by Bioscience Laboratory that had analyzed specimens taken during the postmortem on Elvis. The report indicated that Elvis's death was the result of polypharmacy, or the interaction of several drugs taken at the same time. A few days later, *The New York Times* ran a story that backed Rivera's findings.

In 1980, Elvis's physician, Dr. George Nichopolous, had his medical license suspended for three months and was placed on three years probation. In 1981, Nichopolous was charged with 14 counts of "willingly and feloniously" overprescribing drugs to Elvis. He was acquitted, but many people came to view him as a villain. During a football game in Memphis in 1979, someone took a shot at Nichopolous but missed.

The spontaneous outpouring of grief over Elvis's death, the extended coverage by the news media, and the offering of condolences from around the world was reminiscent of the mourning that occurs when a head of state dies. Hundreds of editorials attempted to summarize Elvis's place in our culture. For the first time, the nation as a whole seemed to realize that Elvis had changed the way we look, the music we listen to, the way we talk, and the kind of hero we believe in.

At the time, many people felt that Elvis's death marked the end of an era, as well as the end of a legendary career, but this has not proved to be true. After Elvis died, the mythology surrounding him continued to grow with each new revelation about his personal life and each new reinterpretation of his contribution to popular culture. Elvis the man died on August 17, 1977, but Elvis the myth continues to flourish. The King is dead; long live the King.

Opposite page: A statue commemorating Elvis was sculpted by Eric Parks and erected in Memphis in 1980.

CHAPTER TEN

LONG LIVE THE KING

"ELVIS, I FONDLE YOUR HAIR IN MY DREAMS."

—*Graffiti on the wall at Graceland*

Elvis experienced an extraordinary 23-year career in show business. He was an artistic and financial success, and he made an enormous impact on the history of popular music. Since his death, Elvis has continued to generate revenue for his estate, his popularity among his fans has not diminished, and each new piece of information about his personal life serves to keep his name in the news. The word most often associated with this continued interest and unwavering support is "phenomenon."

Key to the Elvis phenomenon is the loyalty of his fans. His death left a void that fans have filled with conventions, rituals, fan clubs, and other activities. Their intense devotion results from a complex combination of circumstances beginning with Elvis's early career on the country-western circuit. Country music followers are among the most loyal of popular music fans. Many people who love country music remain devoted to a particular performer for decades, and they often inspire their children to become fans as well. Many of Elvis's most devoted fans became interested in him when he was considered a country singer, and they remained loyal to him after he became a national rock 'n' roll star.

Elvis always tried to give his fans what they wanted to see and hear. In the 1950s, his audience came to see his notorious performing style, hoping that he would go farther at each appearance than he'd ever gone before. Elvis was able to whip his audiences into a frenzy, which was an experience not understood by those who were not his fans. In the 1960s, his fans paid to see Elvis's musical films, even though some of these vehicles were badly produced. Although Elvis may have wanted to be a serious actor when he went to Hollywood, his attempts at dramatic acting were not successful at the box office, and Colonel Parker was able to persuade Elvis to continue to make musical comedies by telling him that this was the kind of movie his fans wanted to see. In the 1970s, audiences expected Elvis to perform certain songs, wear his trademark jumpsuits, and strike specific poses—standard parts of his act that he maintained for his fans until he died.

The playful, sometimes sexually charged interaction between Elvis and the audience members during his performances is another

The key to Elvis's continued popularity is the loyalty of his fans. Many have followed his career since the 1950s.

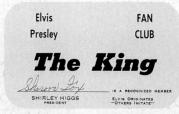

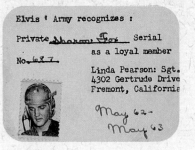

factor in the deep devotion of the fans—at least those who were lucky enough to see him in concert. Elvis liked to single out certain women in his audience and perform specifically for them, breaking down the usual barriers between performer and spectator. Throwing towels into the audience and tossing his capes or personal jewelry into the crowd also contributed to breaking down these barriers, and his fans responded in kind by throwing underwear, keys, flowers, and stuffed animals onto the stage. The result of these interactions and exchanges was an unusually close bond between audience and entertainer. Elvis's fans went to concerts not only to see him perform but also to have personal contact with their idol. Even if all of the fans did not have an opportunity to touch him or to commune with him one to one, they could live vicariously through those who were able to get close to Elvis.

Elvis, the Colonel, and members of Elvis's family always treated the fans with the utmost consideration from the early days of his success until the very end, when Vernon allowed fans to have the flowers from Elvis's funeral. Elvis believed that his success was dependent on his fans, and he was always grateful for their loyalty and love. When he was young, he allowed them access to his personal life in a

Above left: Fans have always gathered in front of the Music Gates. While Elvis was alive, they sometimes waited there, hoping to see him as he drove through.
Above: A sampling of membership cards indicates the diversity of Elvis fan clubs over the years.

In one of Colonel Tom Parker's endless promotion gimmicks during the 1950s, fans were given placards that read "Presley for President" and then paraded before photographers.

Elvis's fan clubs were always treated well by the Presley family and the Colonel. Parker frequently gave special premiums to fan clubs and donated personal Presley paraphernalia for club benefits.

Modern-day fans sometimes become collectors, thereby preserving certain memorabilia that illustrates important details of Elvis's career.

way that no other entertainer would dare. Before Elvis moved to Graceland, fans were always hanging around the Presleys' home. At Graceland, fans often gathered at the gate, and Elvis would walk or ride one of his horses down to sign autographs. Elvis's Uncle Vester, who was one of the guards at the gate house, sometimes stood and talked with fans for hours.

No matter how difficult the fans made Elvis's life by forcing him to live in seclusion, he never complained publicly, and he always had nice things to say to the press about his fans. Colonel Tom Parker gave premiums and special offers to Elvis's fan clubs and donated Elvis's personal belongings to be auctioned off for charity. Elvis once presented a car to the president of one of his fan clubs. When he was on tour during the 1950s, Elvis gave as many interviews to reporters for high-school newspapers and fan-club newsletters as he did to reporters who worked for big-city papers.

Though Elvis accumulated great wealth and success during his lifetime, he never forgot that he was a Southern boy from humble beginnings. He chose not to reside permanently in Hollywood but preferred to live in Memphis, where he frequented local businesses and contributed generously to local charities. Elvis never completely lost his Southern accent, and he always preferred down-home cooking and the company of other good ol' boys. Despite his money, position, and power, he never acted as though he was better than his fans. To fans, this type of information meant that Elvis had always been one of them—one of the people. "I guess you could

say Elvis was what we'd like to be. He's one of us—and yet he's our ideal," said an anonymous fan on one occasion, as though she were speaking for all fans.

Elvis Presley fans have always been intensely devoted, and many have passed that veneration onto other generations as a legacy. Elvis's fans are the most genuine testimony to his talent and impact on all of us.

Since his death, the fans' desire to get close to Elvis is gratified through visiting Graceland, where the events of Elvis's personal life unfolded. Within the walls of Graceland, fans listen to the echoes of Elvis's past that linger in the rooms and halls of his private retreat.

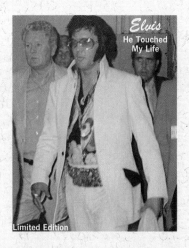

Above: In her self-published book, fan Sharon Fox explains the impact Elvis had on her life.
Below: Fans gather each year in August to remember Elvis Presley and to celebrate his life.

Above right: The fans' desire to remain close to Elvis is gratified through visiting his home, Graceland. **Below right:** A view of the back of the mansion shows some of the changes that Elvis had made. **Opposite page:** Graceland was placed on the National Register of Historic Places in 1991.

Graceland was opened to the public for the first time on June 7, 1982, and it was placed on the National Register of Historic Places in 1991. Graceland was not just Elvis's home, it was his refuge from the pressures of making movies, recording music, and touring in concert. Having endured the death of his mother, his divorce from Priscilla, and two major career changes, Elvis found that Graceland was the only constant in his life. When Graceland was opened to the public, fans finally got the opportunity to see beyond those famous gates with the musical notes.

Until Elvis was inducted into the army, Vernon and Gladys lived in the main house at Graceland. Sadly, Gladys lived there for only a year and a half before she died in August 1958. When Elvis and his family returned from Germany after his discharge, Vernon and his new wife, Dee, lived in another house nearby. A downstairs bedroom in Graceland was used by Elvis's grandmother, Minnie Mae Presley, until she died in 1980. It's now occupied by Elvis's aunt, Delta Mae Biggs, who at one time kept house at Graceland. Over the years, many other relatives and buddies lived in Graceland or on the grounds. According to the terms of his will, Elvis left everything to Vernon, Minnie Mae, and his only child, Lisa Marie, with Vernon and Priscilla Presley as executors. After Vernon and Minnie Mae died, Lisa Marie was to inherit Graceland on her twenty-fifth birthday. When Lisa did inherit the Presley estate in 1993, she decided to keep the current management team in place and take a role in the estate's operations. Her intentions include keeping Graceland open to the public.

There are no antiques at Graceland; there is no decor reminiscent of an earlier era. All of the furnishings are distinctly modern in style. The dire poverty of Elvis's childhood left him with a lifelong hatred of anything old. As he put it, "When I was growing up in Tupelo, I lived with enough…antiques to do me for a lifetime." But contrary to some reports, all of Graceland is not tasteless or tacky. The house is ostentatious, even flamboyant, but the interior design of the main floor is no different from what was found in the homes of many wealthy Southerners in the 1950s and 1960s.

The main floor houses the living room, the dining room, and the music room. These rooms are decorated with white or gilt-edged furniture, silky fabrics, elaborate drapes, crystal chandeliers, marble or mirror paneling, and wall-to-wall carpeting. Most of the walls are white as is the carpeting. The accessories in the dining room are blue, which was Elvis's favorite color, and trimmed in gold. In 1974, Linda Thompson, Elvis's girlfriend at that time, had the accessories changed to bright red, but when Graceland was opened to the public, Elvis's family returned them to their original color. The living room features a stained glass peacock designed for Elvis by Laukhuff Stained Glass of Memphis in 1974. Elvis supposedly liked peacocks because they symbolize eternal life, though superstition has it that displaying peacocks inside a home will bring bad luck. The music room is predominantly gold and now contains a black Story and Clark piano. The piano is one of three that were used at Graceland over the years. The piano that was there the longest was a white and gold baby grand, which was

Priscilla and Lisa Marie reside in California. Lisa inherited the Presley estate in 1993, but she chose to retain the current management and keep Graceland open to the public.

Above left: The massive chandelier in the dining room of Graceland was purchased by Elvis in 1974 on an after-hours shopping spree. **Below left:** The 15-foot white couch and 10-foot coffee table in the living room were custom-made for Elvis.

Above right: The large white monkey on the glass coffee table in the TV room is one of the many seventies-looking details that visitors find charming about the downstairs rooms at Graceland.
Below right: According to official Graceland accounts, the pool table in the pool room dates back to when Elvis purchased the house in 1957.

replaced by a grand piano that Priscilla had covered with gold leaf for Elvis as an anniversary gift. The gold piano proved too large for the room, according to official accounts from the Presley estate, and it was replaced by the black Story and Clark.

The rooms designed for Elvis's personal use are more flamboyant and personalized than the other rooms in Graceland. The TV room, which was decorated in its present style in 1974, features mirrors on the ceiling and a wrap-around mirrored bar with an old-fashioned soda fountain. A built-in juke box from the 1950s fills one corner of the room. Much of Elvis's personal record collection is housed here, with some discs dating back to his high-school days. The focal point of the room is the bank of three televisions that are set side by side in a wall unit. Elvis got the idea for this arrangement from President Lyndon Johnson, who liked to watch the news simultaneously on all three networks. The TV room is predominantly navy blue and gold, with a supergraphic of a TCB lightning bolt emblazoned on one wall.

The pool room is across the hall from the TV room. It's decorated with about 350 to 400 yards of patchwork-printed fabric draped on both the walls and ceiling. A large stained glass lamp by Laukhuff Stained Glass hangs over the pool table, where Elvis enjoyed playing his favorite billiard game, eight ball. Interior designer Bill Eubanks helped decorate some of the rooms at Graceland, including the pool room and the TV room, but Elvis was always specific about how he wanted a room to look. Elvis selected most of the fabrics and furniture for Graceland, although he occasionally got help from people whose opinions he trusted.

The jungle room was Elvis's favorite. The 40-foot-long room contains massive pieces of heavy furniture with fake-fur upholstery. The story goes that after Elvis saw a commercial for a Memphis furniture store called Donald's, he decided on the spur of the moment to drive down to the store and take a look at what was in stock. Within 30 minutes, he'd selected and purchased enough furniture for the entire jungle room. Everything was delivered that same day. In other versions of the story, Vernon was the first to hear of Donald's, and he began to talk about their strange furniture to Elvis and his buddies. Elvis had already seen the furniture and decided to buy it, much to Vernon's dismay.

The room is decorated in a Tahitian or Hawaiian motif, with hand-carved thrones and varnished, scallop-edged Cypress tables, accented with wooden lamps carved to resemble angry gods. By the time Elvis created his tropical paradise, the room already had green shag rugs on the ceiling and a built-in waterfall with colored lights.

If the decor of the house reveals Elvis Presley the man, then the trophy room behind Graceland heralds Elvis the legend. Located in a separate building just south of the main house, the trophy room contains a vast collection of Elvis memorabilia, from his seventh grade achievement test to his many gold and platinum records. Also on view in the trophy room are many of the jeweled jumpsuits Elvis wore in the 1970s, the black brocade tuxedo and white wedding dress in which Elvis and Priscilla were married, and some of his

Above right: The ceiling of the jungle room is carpeted, which was a fad during the 1970s. When Elvis decided to use the room for rehearsals and, later, recording, the carpeted ceilings proved to be acoustically beneficial. **Below right:** The "Hall of Gold," located in the trophy room, displays Elvis's gold and platinum records as well as other awards.

favorite jewelry. A wall display of Elvis's firearms and police badges hangs near a glass case that holds two of the three Grammy Awards he won for his inspirational recordings. Fans are represented in the trophy room through the displays of letters requesting that Elvis not be drafted, by the eccentric gifts sent to him over the years, and by the condolence telegrams sent from around the world when he died. The trophy room houses items that are both compelling and trivial, priceless and worthless, poignant and bizarre.

The emotional high point of any visit to Graceland is Elvis's grave in Meditation Gardens behind the main house. A brick and white-columned peristyle encloses the small space in which Elvis, his parents, and his grandmother are buried. At the head of Elvis's grave burns an eternal flame, which sits atop a marble base marked by a bronze plaque. The plaque bears a touching epitaph written by his father, Vernon, a quiet man who rarely expressed himself regarding the extraordinary life and times of his famous offspring. Vernon finally bared his feelings in this poignant inscription in which he remembered his son as "A precious gift from God."

Each year on the anniversary of Elvis's death, thousands of fans brave the sweltering August heat in Memphis to remember their idol. They have organized a week of tributes and memorials that includes visiting Graceland, Sun Records, and other Presley haunts. The week culminates in a candlelight ceremony. This ritual has been enacted every year since Elvis's death. On the evening of August 15, fans gather in front of the Music Gate. They sing some of Elvis's songs and

Top: Vernon Presley remembers his son a year after his death. **Bottom:** Meditation Gardens.

217

Above and above right: Each August during the week that marks the anniversary of Elvis's death, fans pay their respects by visiting Graceland and viewing Elvis's grave. **Right:** A bronze plaque was placed near the entrance of Meditation Gardens to remember Elvis's twin brother, Jessie, who died at birth.

IN MEMORY OF
JESSIE GARON PRESLEY
JANUARY 8, 1935

Left and below left: The candle-light ceremony is the culmination of the week-long commemoration and celebration that is referred to by fans as Elvis Week.

219

Above, above right, right, and opposite page: During Elvis Week, thousands of flower arrangements and memorial pieces pour into Graceland from fan clubs around the world. Some are hand-crafted.

220

Above: Manufacturers and merchandisers mark the anniversary of Elvis's death with various commemorative items. **Far right:** The merchandising of the singer began as far back as 1956 when the Colonel made a deal to slap Elvis's name and face on everything from tennis shoes to lipstick.

swap Elvis stories. At 11:00 P.M., two or more Graceland employees walk down to the gate with a torch that has been lighted from the eternal flame. As the Music Gate swings open, the fans, each with their own lighted candle, climb silently and reverently up the hill behind the house, where they walk single file past the grave site. The procession often takes as long as six hours to pass through Meditation Gardens. It is not only a gesture of respect for Elvis and what he represents, but it's also proof that Elvis's fans are as faithful after his death as they were during his lifetime.

The fans aren't alone in remembering the anniversary of Elvis's death. Each year merchandisers, promoters, collectors, and manufacturers who market and sell commemorative items and souvenirs mark the passing of another year. Significant dates, such as the tenth anniversary of Elvis's death or his fiftieth birthday, increase the amount of Elvis merchandise that goes on sale. The diversity of this merchandise is overwhelming and often amusing. From clothing to shampoo, from liquor decanters to lamps, from board games to dolls, it's difficult to find any kind of product that hasn't been transformed into an Elvis souvenir, memento, or collectible. Even dirt from the grounds of Graceland and sweat (supposedly) from Elvis's body have been sold. The enormous variety of these collectibles and the crass commercialism behind some of them have attracted a lot of attention. Catalogs of Elvis merchandise are available, and newspaper features and television news stories have spotlighted collectors of Elvis memorabilia.

Though fans accept this aspect of the phenomenon and take it in stride, the press seems obsessed with the marketing of Elvis, often focusing their commentary on those offbeat items deemed to be in bad taste. The implication is that Elvis is being exploited in death through the proliferation of outlandish merchandise bearing his name and image. Yet, the marketing of Elvis Presley began a long time ago. As far back as 1956, Colonel Parker negotiated with promoter Henry G. Saperstein for the rights to manufacture products with Elvis's picture on them. In the 1950s, Elvis's name and face showed up on lipstick (Tutti Frutti Red and Hound Dog Orange), charm bracelets, jeans, hats, and even women's panties.

After Elvis died, Parker continued to manage the star's business. Legend has it that minutes after he heard about Elvis's death, Parker

muttered, "Nothing has changed. This won't change anything." By the time Elvis was buried, Parker had made a deal with Factors, Inc., to market Elvis products. The Colonel got Vernon Presley's signature to seal the deal on the day of Elvis's funeral.

In 1980, the executors of Elvis's estate, including Priscilla Presley (Vernon had died in 1979), petitioned the court for approval of all the financial transactions made with Parker on behalf of the estate for the purposes of establishing a trust fund. A court-appointed attorney, Blanchard E. Tual, investigated Parker's management of Elvis from the begin-ning of his career to Parker's final deal with Factors, Inc. This inquiry resulted in a court case charging Parker with "enriching himself by mismanaging Presley's career." The judge ordered the Presley estate to stop all dealings with Parker and to sue him to recover at least part of the money the Colonel was responsible for losing. In 1983, the estate attempted to sue Parker, who sought dismissal of the lawsuit on the grounds that he was not an American citi-zen and could not be sued under federal laws. For the first time, the Colonel admitted that he was born Andreas Cornelius van Kuijk in Holland and had never been a U.S. citizen.

Below left: Licensed Presley collectibles include liquor decanters that represent different phases of his career. **Below:** A number of Elvis dolls have been marketed in the years since his death.

In 1978, Joseph Rascoff, a business manager for Elvis's estate, said, "A whole industry was built around an animated mouse named Mickey. The next could be Elvis Presley." Judging from the products shown here, his statement proved to be true.

The case was settled out of court. In 1984, Tennessee law established that the Presley estate controlled the rights to Elvis Presley's name and likeness, and that all royalties shall go to the estate.

More important than the souvenirs, merchandise, and commemoratives is the music of Elvis Presley, which has been overshadowed by the more peculiar aspects of the phenomenon generated since his death. Before he died in 1977, Elvis sold 250 million records worldwide. Immediately after his death, record stores across the country quickly sold out of Elvis's records. RCA's pressing plants operated 24 hours a day to fill the new orders for Elvis's records that began to pour in. For a while, the record company subcontracted other pressing plants to keep up with the demand. By September, RCA still had not caught up with all of the orders. RCA's offices and pressing plants outside the U.S. found themselves in the same position. Pressing plants operated day and night. One factory in Hamburg, West Germany, produced only Elvis records in an attempt to meet the demands. By October, sales were so high in the U. S. that several of Elvis's albums were on the charts again.

Though Elvis was dead, RCA continued to release albums of his music at the rate of two or three per year. As was the case while he was alive, some of the albums were well-received, others were criticized for their inferior quality. The marketing strategy behind the albums varied as much as their quality. Some albums, such as *Guitar Man*, attempted to take advantage of contemporary recording techniques to "improve" Elvis's sound. Other albums, such

as *He Walks Beside Me—Favorite Songs of Faith and Inspiration*, contained previously released material repackaged for yet another time. Still other albums seemed to be the result of RCA searching the vaults for any recording of Elvis's voice. *Elvis—Greatest Hits Vol. 4*, for example, contained previously released cuts in addition to never-before-released "live" material from Las Vegas, Hawaii, and Nashville.

In 1983, a record producer from RCA found master tapes and records stored at Graceland, some of which contained unreleased live performances and offstage conversations with Elvis. In 1985, RCA released much of the musical material on a six-album set that celebrated Elvis's fiftieth birthday.

Elvis's most important legacy is his music. **Top left:** For *Our Memories of Elvis*, which featured Vernon Presley and Colonel Parker on the cover, none of the songs were over-dubbed by RCA. **Top:** After Elvis's death, this 1974 album recharted for 14 weeks. **Above left:** Released in 1978, this album was a repackaged collection of songs with religous themes. Two of the cuts were takes that had never been released. **Above:** This songless EP features interviews with Elvis just prior to leaving for the army.

Several bootleg albums of specific concerts have been issued since Elvis died. This two-record bootleg was recorded at Elvis's 1976 New Year's Eve concert in Pittsburgh.

RCA has been criticized by purists for tinkering with the recordings of their most famous artist. Over the years RCA has released several Elvis Presley albums of older material that has been cleaned up for modern audiences. *I Was the One* makes use of modern instruments that were overdubbed to accompany his vocals. Other albums consisted of original mono recordings with "rechanneled stereo." Rock 'n' roll historians claim any attempt to "improve" or "clean up" Elvis's early recordings does not illuminate his contributions to popular music; instead, it distorts them.

A new approach to marketing and releasing Elvis Presley's music began after RCA was sold to a German publishing group called Bertlesmann Music Group in 1986. BMG formed an international restoration committee two years later to research and restore the Presley catalog of recordings. Representatives from America, England, Germany, Denmark, and Asia comprised the committee, which was ultimately responsible for the high quality of *Elvis: The King of Rock 'n' Roll—The Complete '50s Masters* and *From Nashville to Memphis: The Essential '60s Masters, Vol. 1*. These two sets of CDs represent a faithful audio document of Elvis's music from the 1950s and 1960s. The tracks have been digitally remastered from old Sun and RCA recordings, but they maintain the integrity of the originals. Also included are the original vocal exchanges and patter between Elvis and his musicians. The inclusion reveals that Elvis was very much in charge of many of his recording sessions, serving as his own producer.

The BMG committee also researched the actual sales figures for the records and albums that Elvis sold. The Recording Industry Association of America (RIAA) is the official organization to which record companies report sales and request gold and platinum records for their artists. However, the RIAA was not formed until 1958, and Elvis had already sold millions of records by then. Though RCA awarded Elvis various in-house gold records for his pre-1958 hits, they never asked the RIAA for retroactive certification of these records. Also, RCA rarely requested additional certification when Elvis's records went gold or platinum more than once. The BMG committee used Colonel Tom Parker's files to accurately research just how many records Elvis sold and which ones deserved gold, platinum, or multiplatinum status. After completing their research, they estimated that Elvis Presley has sold over a billion records worldwide. By August of 1992, the committee had updated the status of Elvis's albums and singles. As a result, he was awarded 110 additional gold, platinum, and multiplatinum albums and singles by the RIAA—the largest presentation of gold and platinum records in history.

The almost continuous release of controversial biographical information about Elvis keeps his name in the news and fuels the phenomenon. Immediately following his death and perhaps in response to *Elvis: What Happened?*, biographies by former employees began to appear. Some of these books vehemently denied that Elvis abused drugs or showed signs of erratic behavior. Even though these biographies claimed to be inside stories, the books that focused on Elvis's saintly behavior were written by employees who actually had little day-to-day contact with him. *My Life with Elvis* by Becky Yancey and Cliff Linedecker claims to be the "fond memories of a fan who became Elvis's private secretary." The book relates several lighthearted anecdotes about Elvis, including how Yancey met him: She threw up on him after riding a roller coaster. May Mann, a former Hollywood gossip columnist extolled Elvis's virtues in her book, *Elvis, Why Won't They Leave You Alone?* She claimed that she wrote her book because Elvis asked her to; he wanted Lisa Marie to know the truth.

Members of the Memphis Mafia also published books about Elvis. Jerry Hopkins wrote *Elvis: The Final Years,* while Marty and Patsy Lacker collaborated on *Elvis: Portrait of a Friend.* Both confirm the stories from *Elvis: What Happened?* about Elvis's drug use and destructive lifestyle. It was as though a battle line had been drawn between the people who had known Elvis personally: On one side were friends and employees who insisted in books

 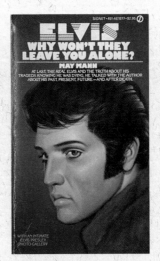 

and interviews that there was only a "good Elvis"; on the other side were people who accepted that he also had his bad habits and characteristics.

By the 1980s, professional writers and scholars began to publish books about Elvis. Albert Goldman's 1981 biography *Elvis* remains the most notorious account of Elvis's life. In addition to his drug problems, Goldman's mean-spirited biography speculated that Elvis had an unhealthy attachment to his mother as well as to his friends in the Memphis Mafia. He also described in detail certain aspects of Elvis's bizarre lifestyle, including his eating habits and his dangerous games with firearms. Rock-music historian Dave Marsh's eloquent *Elvis,* published in the same year, concentrates on the singer's contributions to popular music and culture. His insightful book serves as a counterpoint to Goldman's harsh, biased view.

Later biographies by members of Elvis's family acknowledged his bad side but most often balanced these stories with anecdotes

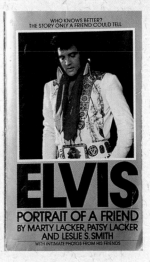

Far left and above: After the release of *Elvis: What Happened,* cowritten by Red West (FAR LEFT), several other books by Elvis's friends and employees were published.

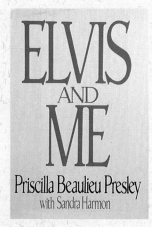

ELVIS AND ME

Priscilla Beaulieu Presley
with Sandra Harmon

Above and above right: Priscilla Presley's biography, *Elvis and Me*, was published in 1985.
Below and below right: Elvis's stepbrothers, Rick and David Stanley, have coauthored and authored several books about their relationship with Elvis.

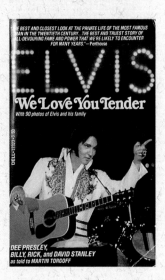

about his generosity. The most awaited biography was Priscilla Beaulieu Presley's account of her relationship with Elvis, titled *Elvis and Me*. Published in 1985, the book offers no revelations about his career, but it does provide some much-needed insight into his secluded lifestyle during the 1960s. *The Touch of Two Kings* by Elvis's stepbrother Rick Stanley, who is now a minister, recounts Stanley's experiences with his famous relative. *Elvis: We Love You Tender* by his stepmother Dee Stanley is a compassionate look at Elvis's ups and downs during the 1960s and 1970s. In 1990, David Stanley, Rick's brother, was interviewed by Albert Goldman in regard to Elvis's death.

David supposedly convinced Goldman that Elvis had committed suicide by intentionally overdosing on drugs. Goldman's account of David Stanley's unsubstantiated claims appeared in *Life* magazine. The following year, Goldman's extended version of this highly speculative account of Elvis's death was published in a book titled *Elvis: The Last 24 Hours,* touching off a wave of protest from fans.

In 1987, Lucy de Barbin published a colorful account of her love affair with Elvis entitled *Are You Lonesome Tonight?* De Barbin claimed that in 1956 Elvis fathered one of her daughters. The book gained wide exposure when it was syndicated in a national magazine, but any controversy it may have caused was quickly overshadowed by a rash of unusual rumors proposing that Elvis was still alive.

Initially, the rumors that Elvis Presley had faked his own death served to discredit his standing as an important cultural figure. Around 1987, after years of negative publicity about his drug abuse and self-destructive lifestyle, the career of Elvis Presley was finally being re-evaluated. To mark the tenth anniversary of his death, a reappraisal of his musical contributions began surfacing in the popular press. But, this appreciation was short-lived because as soon as rumors regarding the possibility that Elvis was still alive surfaced, any credible assessment of his career was completely undermined. Elvis Presley quickly became the target of ridicule in national magazines and the subject of jokes in the media.

Fueled by Gail Brewer-Giorgio's self-published book entitled *The Most Incredible Elvis Presley Story Ever Told* and a song by Texas record producer Major Bill Smith called "Hey! Big E," the "Elvis is alive" rumors escalated in 1988 with reported sightings of Elvis in fast-food restaurants in Michigan. Giorgio's book was republished as *Is Elvis Alive?* to take advantage of the media attention surrounding the current surge of interest in Elvis. As proof of her incredible claim that Elvis is alive, an audiocassette of Elvis's voice was included with each of her books. The cassette featured a voice that sounded like Elvis Presley's discussing certain events that occurred after he died. An Elvis sound-alike later came forward declaring that he had made the recording for a project that never materialized, a claim Giorgio naturally denied.

Ultimately, the authenticity of the tape and the holes in Giorgio's theories mattered very little, because the rumors and the way they were handled in the popular press added another dimension to the Elvis Presley phenomenon. The frequency of books, newspaper and tabloid articles, and programs on radio and television indicated that many people—whether or not they believed the rumors—were interested in keeping Elvis Presley "alive." Bumper stickers that sentimentally declared, "Elvis lives in my heart," were replaced with the more emphatic, "Elvis Lives." But, it was not the historical Elvis Presley that was resurrected—it was Elvis the icon of American popular culture. The "Elvis is alive" stories and the massive amounts of publicity that surrounded their circulation helped refigure the historical Elvis into an American folk hero endowed with as much symbolic signficance as Davy Crocket or Wyatt Earp. As an icon, Elvis Presley can evoke any number of ideas,

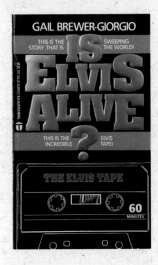

This notorious book by Gail Brewer-Giorgio touched off the "Elvis is alive" rumors in the late 1980s.

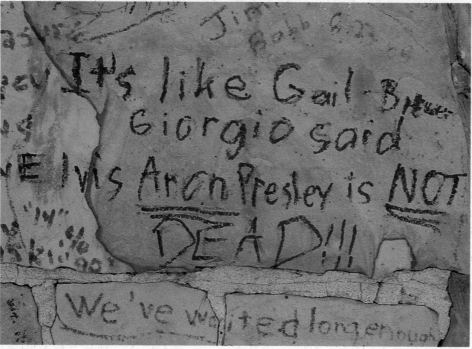

Top and bottom: Fans express their feelings on the stone wall that surrounds Graceland.

including rebellion, success, excessiveness, and the glory and pitfalls of fame. As a folk hero, he inspires the telling and retelling of anecdotes and stories that are exaggerated and manipulated to illustrate any one of these ideas.

The Elvis Presley impersonators are perhaps the most curious offshoot of the collective desire to keep him alive. Elvis impersonators existed long before his death in 1977, but in recent years, imitating Elvis has blossomed into a mini-industry. Some of the impersonators have had plastic surgery to make their faces and bodies resemble the real Elvis as much as possible. Their acts consist entirely of imitating Elvis's singing and performing style, his appearance, and his mannerisms and speech patterns. Most impersonators choose to limit themselves to imitating Elvis as he appeared in Las Vegas, and many of them keep up the ruse when they are offstage. No fans mistake the impersonators for the real Elvis, and no fans expect them to be as talented or charismatic as Elvis, or even to look exactly like him. The impersonators help the fans remember what Elvis was like and help them relive the excitement of one of his live performances.

Hollywood has always loomed large in the ebb and flow of Elvis's career. After his death, various television biographies and documentaries explored different facets of his life, from his personal relationships to his career high points. By the end of the 1980s, a different cinematic depiction of Elvis Presley emerged. Several films included the figure of Elvis not to tell the story of his life but to make use of

Above left: Impersonator Mike Memphis strikes his best Elvis pose. **Below left:** One of the many made-for-TV biographies about Elvis that appeared on the small screen after his death was based on Priscilla's book *Elvis and Me*. In this 1988 mini-series, Dale Midkiff portrayed Elvis; Susan Walters played Priscilla.

the iconographic power of his image to convey a theme or idea, further establishing his identity as a folk hero.

Heartbreak Hotel (1988) features Elvis Presley as a character in a fictionalized tale. Set in 1972, the storyline involves a teenage boy who kidnaps Elvis and brings him home to his single mother in a small Ohio town. The family has its share of problems. They live in a ramshackle boarding house that has fallen into disrepair, which seems to reflect the disorder of their lives. The mother is depressed, lonely, and always falls for the wrong men; the son lacks self-confidence; and the daughter is afraid of the monsters that lurk in the dark. Like a bona fide hero, Elvis "rescues" them from their problems. As he repairs the fixtures on the house, mows the lawn, and even redecorates, he restores order within the family, fixing broken hearts and mending egos. At the same time, Elvis finds happiness in performing these everyday tasks and chores—something he never gets to do as the King of Rock 'n' Roll.

The following year, two films were released that used Elvis Presley as a symbol,

Though he didn't look much like Elvis, David Keith lends an air of playfulness to his portrayal of the famous singer in *Heartbreak Hotel.*

Michael St. Gerard (RIGHT) portrayed Elvis (LEFT) in two feature films and in *Elvis,* the short-lived 1990 television series. The resemblance is striking.

rather than presenting him as a flushed-out character. *Great Balls of Fire* was an interpretive biography of Jerry Lee Lewis, another rockabilly singer who, like Elvis, had started with the Sun record label in Memphis. In the film, Lewis is shown as a rock 'n' roll singer destined to follow in Elvis's footsteps until Lewis's uncompromising nature brings him down. Elvis Presley is used as a symbol of success—the highest level of fame and fortune. Lewis's closeness in achieving that goal is indicated in two scenes involving Elvis. As Lewis's star is rising, Elvis is depicted as being jealous of the adulation of Lewis by his fans. Later, just as Lewis is about to reach the pinnacle of success and Elvis has been drafted, Elvis bitterly tells Jerry Lee, "Take it, take it all."

Heart of Dixie, a drama about racial issues, takes place in Mississippi during the mid-1950s. An Elvis Presley concert is used to illustrate the state of race relations at the time. Elvis's remarkable but volatile music—a combination of white country-western and black rhythm and blues—signifies integration, and, in the film, his concert draws both blacks and whites. Tension over this union of cultures and the mixing of races erupts into violence at the concert when white audience members brutally attack a black couple who are dancing. The situation prefigures the tension that will surface over the announcement about the integration of the University of Mississippi.

Actor Michael St. Gerard portrayed Elvis Presley in both *Great Balls of Fire* and *Heart of Dixie.* When ABC-TV was casting for an actor to portray the famous singer in a series, St. Gerard landed the part once again. The series was short-lived, running only during the spring of 1990, but it offered the public a thought-provoking interpretation of Elvis's life. In doing so, it contributed to his status as a folk or mythic hero. The series, entitled *Elvis,* chronicled Presley's life as a teenager in Memphis at the very beginning of his career. Though the series was based on his real-life experiences, each episode contained a deeper significance. Some episodes were allegories that foretold Elvis's eventual impact on popular music and his legendary status as the King of Rock 'n' Roll; others commented on the effect of his childhood on the rest of his life.

These cinematic representations have focused on the symbolic power of Elvis to evoke ideas and to move us emotionally. No longer just a performer or a famous figure, Elvis Presley, the King of Rock 'n' Roll, can embody a range of emotions, concepts, and values. Given the exploitation of Elvis through merchandising, the inaccuracy of many of the biographies, and the hype that surrounds him even in death, becoming an American folk hero is a more suitable epitaph.

Below and below right: *Elvis,* the television series, not only told the story of the singer's early career it also attempted to portray him as a legendary figure. Actor Michael St. Gerard perfectly captured Elvis's gestures and poses.

 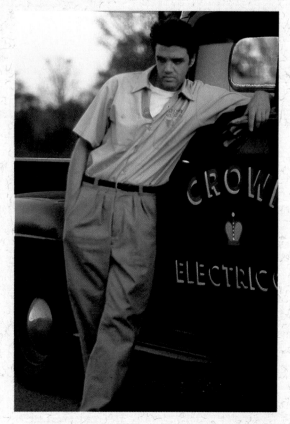

Left: In the TV series *Elvis*, Jesse Dabson (LEFT) played Scotty Moore and Blake Gibbons (CENTER) played Bill Black. **Below left:** The real Moore and Black back Elvis at the 1956 Mississippi-Alabama Fair and Dairy Show.

History books tell us that America has no royalty—no queens, no kings. Yet, we have crowned Elvis "the King of Rock 'n' Roll."

It was a nickname bestowed on him early in his career to imply the financial and popular success he was experiencing in rock 'n' roll music, a style still new to the press and critics. The title has since become the most memorable of his career nicknames, perhaps because metaphors of royalty fit so well with a life and career characterized by kingly accomplishments and excesses.

If Elvis is the King of Rock 'n' Roll, then his kingdom is not easily defined and just as difficult to defend. Many of his subjects are fickle, preferring to follow younger pretenders to the throne. But, almost 20 years after his death, his crown remains intact, only slightly tarnished by the criticism, exploitation, and hype that surrounds the King even in death.

Still, it is a fitting title because it embraces the diversity of Elvis's career and the contradictory images that go with it. From the poor Southern kid who cringed at the nickname "Elvis the Pelvis" to the bona fide American folk hero, "the King of Rock 'n' Roll" embodies all that has been Elvis Presley.

History books tell us that America has no royalty—no queens, no kings. The history books are wrong.

Below: Elvis swings as "Elvis the Pelvis." **Below right:** As the "Million-Dollar Actor," he looked every bit the handsome, mature leading man.

Crowned the "the King of Rock n' Roll" in 1956, Elvis was the very essence of that title to his last day—and beyond.

ADDITIONAL COPYRIGHT
INFORMATION

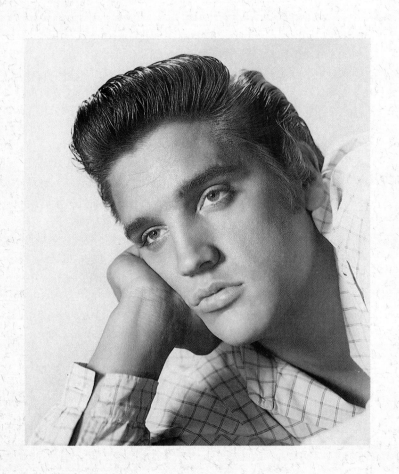